FEAR FIGHTERS

FEAR FIGHTERS

JENTEZEN FRANKLIN

Charisma
HOUSE
A STRANG COMPANY

Most Strang Communications Book Group products are available at special quantity discounts for bulk purchase for sales promotions, premiums, fund-raising, and educational needs. For details, write Strang Communications Book Group, 600 Rinehart Road, Lake Mary, Florida 32746, or telephone (407) 333-0600.

Fear Fighters by Jentezen Franklin
Published by Charisma House
A Strang Company
600 Rinehart Road
Lake Mary, Florida 32746
www.strangbookgroup.com

Unless otherwise noted, all Scripture quotations are from the New King James Version of the Bible. Copyright © 1979, 1980, 1982 by Thomas Nelson, Inc., publishers. Used by permission.

Scripture quotations marked KJV are from the King James Version of the Bible.

Scripture quotations marked NIV are from the Holy Bible, New International Version of the Bible. Copyright © 1973, 1978, 1984, International Bible Society. Used by permission.

Scripture quotations marked THE MESSAGE are from *The Message: The Bible in Contemporary English*, copyright © 1993, 1994, 1995, 1996, 2000, 2001, 2002. Used by permission of NavPress Publishing Group.

Design Director: Bill Johnson
Cover design by Justin Evans

Library of Congress Cataloging-in-Publication Data:
Franklin, Jentezen, 1962-
  Fear fighters / by Jentezen Franklin. -- 1st ed.
     p. cm.
  ISBN 978-1-59979-762-5
  1. Fear--Religious aspects--Christianity. I. Title.
  BV4908.5.F73 2009
  248.4--dc22

                                        2009035033

First Edition

09 10 11 12 13 — 9 8 7 6 5 4 3 2 1
Printed in the United States of America

CONTENTS

1

FACING OFF WITH YOUR FEARS

IT WAS A typical Sunday afternoon in late January. I had finished preaching that morning in my church in Gainesville, Georgia, and was preparing to board a plane with my wife, two of our children, and some staff from our church. We were flying to our pastorate in California to preach to several thousand people who would attend two services later that afternoon. This Sunday afternoon flight to California had become a happy routine since God had opened the door for us to pastor Free Chapel Orange County, our West Coast campus. However, this Sunday would be anything but routine.

Every January at Free Chapel, we begin the year with a twenty-one-day fast. This particular Sunday was special since it was the last day of the fast—which meant we could eat!

We had just begun enjoying our meal when suddenly the cabin of the plane became extremely hot. We reached up to open the air vents, and smoke billowed. Next thing we knew, one of the pilots came out of the cockpit to urge us to put on our masks and brace ourselves because we were on our way down for an emergency landing due to a loss of pressure.

That's when everybody started throwing out their lunch. But not me; this was my first meal in twenty-one days! If this was my final day on this earth, I wasn't going to leave it hungry! I asked the person next to me to pass the ketchup, and I kept on eating. I had one hand on my wife's knee to calm her down, the other hand holding my fork, and my elbow steadying my plate.

Sure I was scared at the thought that something was terribly wrong, but in the midst of my fear, I had peace. Though it was a terrifying situation, I had a calmness in my spirit, and I knew that everything was going to be all right. It wasn't until we landed and the emergency trucks rushed the plane when I realized the magnitude of the situation. I began to praise the Lord for His protection, and I proclaimed to the enemy that he had lost again.

The next week when we were getting ready to board the plane, fear confronted me. In that moment I had a decision to make:

fight the fear and get on board, or give in to fear and give up on God's assignment for my life. That day, my prayer before liftoff was much more earnest than in the past. I began to quote Psalm 91 and claim God's promise of protection. I chose to fight my fear instead of allowing fear to conquer me. And each week, I continue to get on that plane and fly across the country to minister to thousands of people.

I learned a lesson that day. Whenever fear comes my way—and it will come—I have a choice. My faith can fight fear. I don't have to panic and get myself worked up in frightening situations. If I stay focused on God's promise and allow faith to fight fear, He will keep me in perfect peace.

LIVING WITHOUT FEAR

As I considered that phenomenal peace I experienced in what should have been a frightening situation, I began to meditate on the scriptures that promise us a life without fear:

> For God has not given us a spirit of fear, but of power
> and of love and of a sound mind.
> —2 TIMOTHY 1:7

Overcoming fear is something we all face when we endeavor to do new things, such as take a new job, fall in love, create a new product line, or start a business. For example, when we consider where to invest money, we must face the fear of failure. In short, there can be no progress in life without taking risks. You cannot succeed in life if you give in to fear.

The corporate world risks failure every time they launch another high-tech "toy"; the fashion world risks failure with every new line of clothing. Yet, they are willing to take huge, multimillion-dollar risks to improve their merchandise and boost their sales. Do they always win? No. But without taking a risk, they have no chance to succeed.

The business world takes more risks than the average Christian. Why? Because we have to overcome our fear of failure before we can take a calculated risk. What are the consequences of not taking a risk? This amusing story will give you the picture:

> There was a very cautious man
> Who never laughed or played;
> He never risked, he never tried,
> He never sang or prayed.
> And when he one day passed away
> His insurance was denied;
> For since he never really lived,
> They claimed he never died![1]

What a zero! It is impossible to live life without trying new things and taking risks and possibly experiencing failure. We all fail. The failure rate of the human race is 100 percent. Everyone qualifies for membership in the club of failures. That does not mean we have to live in the fear of failure.

If we do not face off with our fears, they will keep us from living the victorious life that God meant for us. And we will suffer the regret of what could have, would have, or should have been.

You will never be perfect. So you will never be perfectly successful. That doesn't mean you will not succeed in life—but you must try.

Afraid to Try?

I heard of a guy who couldn't speak English. He was terrified of trying because he did not want to fail. So he found an English teacher and asked him to teach him how to order a meal in a restaurant in perfect English. The teacher taught him how to say four words: *hamburger, french fries*, and *Coke*.

Every day after that, the man went to order his hamburger, french fries, and Coke. Soon he grew tired of eating the same thing every day. So he asked the English teacher to teach him how to order something else to eat. The teacher taught him to say *eggs, toast*, and *juice*.

So the man went happily to the restaurant to order eggs, toast, and juice. But when the waiter asked, "How do you want your eggs?" the guy stared back blankly. Then the waiter asked, "What kind of toast do you want? And would you like orange juice or apple juice?" The guy stared helplessly at the waiter for a moment and then said, "Hamburger, french fries, Coke."

A lot of people live a "hamburger, french fries, Coke" life because they are not willing to do something imperfectly or try to do something new. They will not face off with their fears and risk failure. Their answer to risk-taking is to play it safe. But you cannot please God by playing it safe, and you cannot succeed in life without taking risks.

When you are so afraid of failure that you don't try, you cannot please God. You cannot "play it safe" and please God. I would rather try to do something for God and fail than not try to do anything. That leads to barrenness and futility of your purpose in life.

Recipe for barrenness

There was a tourist driving through beautiful farmland when he saw an old farmer sitting in a rocking chair on his porch. The tourist stopped to chat with him. As he approached, he saw the man's scraggly beard and noted that he was chewing on a piece of straw. Behind the old farmhouse was seventy-five acres of barren land.

The tourist asked the farmer, "Is that your land?"

"Yep," he replied.

"Well, what are you going to do with it? Are you thinking of growing cotton?"

"Nope. I'm afraid the boll weevils will get it."

"What about corn?"

"No. Locusts will eat the corn," the farmer responded, still chewing on the straw.

"Well, is there anything else you can do with the land? What about raising cattle?"

"I am afraid the price of beef might go down."

"So, what are you going to do with your seventy-five acres of prime farmland?"

"Nothing. I am going to play it safe and do nothing."

Have you ever felt that way? Just wanting to play it safe and do nothing? A lot of people do that with their life potential. If you choose just to play it so safe in life, your potential for success becomes a barren wasteland. If fear rules your life, you will not dare to step out in faith to fulfill your destiny in God. But the Bible says that without faith it is impossible to please God (Heb. 11:6). It is better to risk failure to do what God wants you to do than to do nothing.

We have all experienced fear that makes us want to draw back and play it safe. But people who overcome that fear are those who will make it in life. You have to decide to declare your goals for life in the face of fear. Here is what I do when I am overwhelmed by the next challenge life brings my way.

PREACH TO YOURSELF

When God has asked me to do something that seems impossible for me, I have to preach to myself to defeat the fear and uncertainty that try to control me. When I am faced with an impossible task, when the job feels too big for me and I feel that I am out of my league, I have to preach these three things to myself. They have become my fear fighters. I encourage you to make these declarations over your situation.

1. Jesus is with me, and He has all power.

First, I preach this promise to myself: "Jesus is with me—and all power has been given to Him."

In one of the last conversations Jesus had with His disciples, He revealed to them that all power was given to Him in heaven and on Earth. Then He gave them this promise: "Lo, I am with you always, even to the end of the age" (Matt. 28:18–20).

Jesus had just commanded these men to go to all the world to preach the gospel and make disciples. That must have seemed impossible to men who had never left their homeland. Jesus was telling them to do something that even He, the Christ, had never done.

Actually, the earthly ministry of Jesus never covered much territory geographically. If you have ever visited Israel, you know that. You can travel from village to village easily in a few hours. His headquarters was in Capernaum, and He crossed the Sea of Galilee, but it is really just a lake. You can cross it in an hour.

Jesus never went to foreign soil. He never preached in a foreign nation. And yet He commanded His disciples to go into all the world. He left the whole job of winning the world to Christ to these few men.

Then He went up to heaven on a cloud-filled elevator—"See ya!"—and they were left standing there with a command to do what He never did. Their "impossible" job was to cover the whole earth with the good news of the gospel. But they also had this powerful promise from Jesus: "I am with you always, and I have all power. Wherever you go, I am there, even to the end of the world."

So, when you need to step out in faith for whatever challenge you face, preach to yourself, "Jesus is with me, and He has all power!" Jesus wants you to get that revelation. He is saying, "Hell couldn't keep Me, the grave couldn't hold Me, and demons couldn't trap Me. I am alive!" He looks at you and says, "Don't you back up. Don't you tremble. Don't be afraid! Fear not! I have all power!" All power belongs to God.

Your personal challenge is no greater than that of the disciples to go into all the world and make disciples. Whatever it is that you have to face down, that "it" is not in charge. It has no power over your life. If Jesus is in your life, He has all power over every "it" that you face. We are not immune to fear; we have to face it and become fear fighters.

When I get shaky and feel afraid and overwhelmed, I pull myself aside and start preaching to myself: "Jentezen, straighten up. Quit talking all that negative stuff. Jesus is with you, and all power is in His hands!

Instead of talking fear, start declaring that the same Jesus who was with the three Hebrew boys in the fiery furnace is with you. When Nebuchadnezzar looked into the furnace and said, "Did we not cast three men bound into the midst of the fire?" those around him answered yes. He said, "I see four men...and the form of the fourth is like the Son of God" (Dan. 3:24–25).

FEAR FIGHTER

Jesus is with me, and He has
all power!

I would like to correct him; "Mr. Nebuchadnezzar, He is not *like* the Son of God; He *is* the Son of God, and He is with me in my fiery furnace!" He has all power!

So, when you are afraid to take a risk, the first thing you need to preach to yourself is, "Jesus is with me everywhere I go, and all power is in His hands!" That promise has become my number one fear fighter.

When your kids are in crisis, Jesus is with you! When you face overwhelming challenges in finances, Jesus is with you! When you face challenges in the ministry, Jesus is with you! And He has all power in His hands!

2. God is at the bottom.

The second thing I have learned to preach to myself is that no matter how low the trials of life take me, *God is at the bottom.* When I feel I have hit rock bottom and that the challenges are too great to overcome, God is there.

Moses talked to Israel at the close of his life about how great God is. In a kind of national address, he told them that there was no God like their God and that He rides the heavens to help them (Deut. 33:26). He described a God who is on top, above all, on high, a God who is great and mighty.

Do you remember the mighty miracles that God did on mountaintops? It was on Mount Moriah that God met with Abraham and Isaac and made His covenant of the blood of the lamb. On Mount Horeb Moses encountered the burning bush. It was on Mount Sinai that God gave the Ten Commandments. And on Mount Nebo Moses looked across and saw the Promised Land. It was on Mount Carmel that God sent fire down for Elijah.

God is a God of the high places; He is the God of mountaintop experiences. But Moses made a shift in focus right in the middle of telling about this great God of the high places. It is as though he was thinking, "I can't leave the people with the thought that

God is only on top. He is not only with people when everything is victory, when everything is going right."

Then he said, "The eternal God is your refuge, and underneath are the everlasting arms" (Deut. 33:27). The Hebrew word for "underneath" means "bottom." So it could be translated, "God's arms are underneath you at the bottom." No matter how deep the valley you have to walk, God's presence is deeper. His arms are underneath you...at the bottom.

We all know that God is at the top. But what you need to preach to yourself when you are facing off with fear and difficulty is that God is with you when you are at the bottom! You may look like you are down, but you cannot go so low in despair or depression, trouble or sorrow, that He is not there. When you feel that you can go no lower, underneath are His everlasting arms. God is not just the God of the top; He is also the God of the bottom!

I have learned that underneath the ministry He has given us are the everlasting arms of God. Underneath any crisis my family faces are the everlasting arms of God. Jesus is with me, and He has all power—not just when I am on top. God is underneath me, no matter how deep the challenge of trouble or pain. That comforting truth is my second fear fighter: God is at the bottom!

I encourage you to make it your fear fighter as well. You may feel as though you are in a free fall sometimes. Financially you may be facing ruin. Your family may be about to tear apart. You may have lost your best friend. Life may not seem worth living. When you feel as though you are at rock bottom, begin to look for God in that place.

> ## FEAR FIGHTER
>
> God is not just the
> God of the top; He is also the
> God of the bottom!

Let your faith declare that God is at the bottom. Underneath your lowest point, the arms of God are waiting to hold you up. When the dust settles, you will hear God say, "Hi there. Lo, I am with you always!"

3. God has given to everyone a measure of faith.

The third thing I preach to myself is the truth of God's Word that says, "God has dealt to each one a measure of faith" (Rom. 12:3). There is nothing that God will require of me for which I don't have the faith. He has given me the measure of faith I need to please Him. So whatever the challenge I am facing, I preach to myself, "I have faith for this."

Isaiah prophesied that God declares the beginning from the end and from ancient times things that are not yet done (Isa. 46:10). God establishes your end and then goes back to you to say, "OK, let's begin. If you stay in faith, you will walk in My plan for your life because it is already established. I established your end from the beginning."

God has given you the faith you need to begin to walk in His will. Jesus is with you, and He has all power. So when fear threatens your victory, preach three simple truths about faith to yourself: Faith is important. It doesn't take huge faith. I have faith for this.

Faith is important.

First, faith is important. Jesus said to Simon Peter, "Simon, Simon! Indeed, Satan has asked for you, that he may sift you as wheat. But I have prayed for you, that your faith should not fail" (Luke 22:31–32). That was the most important prayer Jesus could pray for Simon.

It is the most important prayer for you also. Not a prayer that you would have the best financial year of your life. Not that you have a life without trouble or problems. But prayer that your faith does not fail.

Faith is more important than money. It is more important than a successful career. It is more important than happiness. Why? Because if you take everything I have but leave me with my faith, I will be back! Faith will connect me to God's will. He is always with me, and He has all power. Failure will never be final if my faith does not fail.

Jesus was saying, in effect, "When Satan is attacking you, the most important prayer that I can pray for you is that your faith will stand through this process you are going through…that your faith will not fail!" Remember first of all that faith is *important*.

It doesn't take huge faith.

The second thing about faith is that you don't have to have a lot of it to live victoriously. Jesus said that faith the size of a mustard seed was enough to move a mountain. Then He said that with that kind of faith, nothing would be impossible to you (Matt. 17:20).

The "mustard seed" concept was a phrase used in Jesus's day to describe something insignificant and small. But Jesus elevated it to say that you need only that "insignificant" kind of faith to do the impossible. Don't despise the day of small beginnings. Let your faith work like that little mustard seed.

You see, the tiny mustard seed has an innate power to grow and overcome obstacles to become a mighty tree. It presses up through the dark earth, around rocks, braving storms and avoiding animals and other threats to its life. It is not so much the size of your faith but the quality of faith that you need to succeed.

It just takes "mustard seed" faith to move something from the impossibility column to the possibility column. The only thing standing between your impossibility and your possibility is a mustard seed kind of faith.

I need this little truth about faith. You see, I don't have great faith. Every time we need to expand the ministry, purchase another TV station, or do whatever God says to do, I just take my little grain of mustard seed faith out there. It has to press through the obstacles.

I make the decisions that are needed and feel as though I am obeying God. Then when the bills start coming in, I feel fear rising, and I start praying, "O God, what are we going to have to cut to make this happen?" But instead of giving in to that fear, I begin to preach to myself that Jesus is with me, that He has all power, and that He has given me a measure of faith to do all His will. My mustard seed faith grows a little more and overcomes the fear.

FEAR FIGHTER

I have faith for this.

You need to let your mustard seed faith grow and increase to become a large tree that flourishes and conquers every fear. It is a faith that doesn't give up. Mustard seed faith is unconquerable faith; it is faith that won't quit. Don't quit in the face of adversity. Call on your faith, and watch it overcome every obstacle.

I have faith for this.

The third thing I have learned to preach to myself about faith is, "I have faith for this." This statement is a powerful fear fighter. Because He has given me a measure of faith and He is asking me to do a certain thing, I can trust that I have a mustard seed kind of faith for this. That is what I preach to myself when something impossible threatens to defeat my family or an area of ministry: *I have faith for this.*

When you are facing a bad report from a doctor or your money is acting funny, just say, "I have faith for this." When the devil is showing you a big zero for your future, just laugh at him and say, "Jesus is with me, and He has all power. God is at the bottom, and underneath are His everlasting arms—and I have faith for this."

I pray that you can use these three fear fighters as I do to help you to fight fear effectively. Declare right now:

1. Jesus is with me, and He has all power!
2. God is at the bottom!
3. I have faith for this!

It is not God's will for your life to be ruled by fear—of any kind. Yet fear is one of the greatest evils you must face off with—and win! So, to live a victorious life, you need to take the challenge personally to become a fear fighter. Your faith will overcome your fear when you determine to become a fear fighter.

Of course, the key to living by faith in a world driven by fear is to submit your life to the lordship of Christ. As you seek first the kingdom of God and His righteousness (Matt. 6:33), you will be restored to intimate relationship with God. Then you can learn to fight fear with the promises of God's Word.

To be an effective fear fighter, you will need God's arsenal of divine weapons—His fear fighters. Without these divine weapons, you cannot defeat fear. As a valiant fear fighter, you will learn to use God's fear fighters to win against every kind of fear.

It is impossible to discuss every divine weapon in God's arsenal. You can trust the Holy Spirit to teach you to become effective in facing off with your fears. As you progress, you will discover more and more divine weapons in the Word of God to use against the power of fear that torments your life.

To begin, I suggest that you use the "Fear Fighter's Arsenal," included at the end of each chapter. Then you can develop your own from your personal revelation of the Word of God. Declare His Word in faith, and nothing life throws at you will overwhelm you, defeat you, or cause you to live in fear.

As you take this first step to living a life free from fear, you will discover that many of your worst fears have actually been "much ado about nothing." You will learn to live in the wonderful shelter of safety that God provides for you. If you have decided to learn how to become an effective fear fighter, please pray this prayer with me:

Dear heavenly Father,

I come to You to declare the truth that Jesus is with me, and He has all power. I declare that You are the God at the bottom when I feel like life is over and I cannot go on. I choose to believe that I have faith for this…that You have given me a measure of faith to become an effective fear fighter—and win! I submit my life completely to Your lordship, Jesus. I choose to face off with my fears and learn to use Your supernatural fear fighters to live a life of victory over all fear. Thank You, Lord. Amen.

FEAR FIGHTER'S ARSENAL

Facing Off With Your Fears

But He [Jesus] said to them, "Why are you fearful, O you of little faith?" Then He arose and rebuked the winds and the sea, and there was a great calm.

—MATTHEW 8:26

But immediately Jesus spoke to them, saying, "Be of good cheer! It is I; do not be afraid."

—MATTHEW 14:27

And when the disciples heard it, they fell on their faces and were greatly afraid. But Jesus came and touched them and said, "Arise, and do not be afraid."

—MATTHEW 17:7

As soon as Jesus heard the word that was spoken, He said to the ruler of the synagogue, "Do not be afraid; only believe."

—MARK 5:36

Peace I leave with you, My peace I give to you; not as the world gives do I give to you. Let not your heart be troubled, neither let it be afraid.

—JOHN 14:27

My Personal Fear Fighters

_____

_____

_____

_____

_____

_____

_____

_____

_____

_____

_____

_____

_____

_____

_____

_____

2

MUCH ADO ABOUT NOTHING

FEAR IS NOT rational. It is not based on fact. Researchers have found that 40 percent of the things we worry about *never* happen, and 30 percent are in the past and can't be helped. Another 12 percent of our worry involves the affairs of others and are not even our business. Ten percent of our worry relates to sickness, real or imagined. That leaves only 8 percent of things we worry about that are even *likely* to happen.[1]

The *Wall Street Journal* published an article about the "worry gene" scientists have discovered. Research scientists from Yale have identified a worry gene that may contribute to chronic worry. It is a gene inherited from one's parents. Yet, even these researchers conclude that having inherited a worry gene doesn't mean you can't overcome worry.[2]

The fact is, you don't have to live with anxiety and worry. Worry is low-grade fear. It is interest paid on trouble before it comes due.[3]

In most cases, according to statistics, what we worry about does not happen. The "trouble" we worry about just never comes due.

If I had not overcome the fear of flying that threatened to torment me, I could be "paying interest" on that irrational fear every time I fly. Yet, the likelihood of dying in a plane crash is remote. I would need to fly every day for nineteen thousand years before reaching the probability of experiencing a fatal plane crash.[4] That makes flying one of the safest forms of transportation. In spite of these facts, the fear of flying is one of the six most feared causes of death. It is really much ado about nothing.

"Why This Ado?"

Jairus, a synagogue official, came and fell at the feet of Jesus, begging Him to come and pray for his daughter who was ill. So, Jesus started to go to his home. But while they were on the way, Jairus's servants came and told him his daughter had died. Jesus told this desperate father, "Do not be afraid, only believe" (Mark 5:36).

When they arrived at his home, everyone was weeping and wailing. Jesus asked, "Why . . . this ado?" (v. 39, KJV). The word *ado* can be translated as "commotion," "clamor," or "uproar." Jesus was really saying, "You are making much ado about nothing." Then, Jesus asked everyone to leave the room, and He took the girl by the hand and told her to get up. She awoke and arose to everyone's amazement.

When I read about this wonderful miracle, I realize that Satan tries to get us to focus on our problem and make a great "ado" over it. The problem becomes greater in our minds than the power of lovely Jesus. To the enemy's delight, we choose to make much ado about nothing.

The title of William Shakespeare's famous romantic comedy, *Much Ado About Nothing,* was drawn from this biblical reference. In his play, he develops the theme of deceptive appearances and warns the reader, "Do not judge by appearances, but judge with right judgment" (John 7:24).[5]

FEAR FIGHTER

Worry is interest paid on trouble
before it comes due.

Fear and worry work to deceive you by appearances. How much energy and emotion have you and I wasted over things that never materialize? We lie awake and look at the ceiling at night thinking that this bad thing is going to happen...yet, it never does. It is simply much ado about nothing.

When I first started pastoring, I was overly aware of what people were saying about the church or me. I would worry about what I heard and immediately want to call those involved to keep things from getting out of hand. But I have learned that if there is a crisis brewing, I am going to let it become a crisis before I decide how to handle it. Otherwise, I am not going to spend time worrying about it. It could be much ado about nothing.

I once heard of a guy who was so neurotic about life that when he went to a football game, he thought the team was talking about him every time they went into a huddle. When fear tries to overwhelm you, calm down. It could be much ado about nothing.

Instead of cringing in fear, begin to declare, "Jesus is with me. His plan is working for me, and His Holy Spirit is comforting me. Why should I get all stressed out and feed my worry gene until it causes sickness to my body? I refuse to make much ado about nothing."

OVERCOMING A CULTURE OF FEAR

If you become completely absorbed in worry over your circumstances, you will not even call on Jesus. Learning the worry habit will make you anxious about everything in life, big and small. Satan is a master at getting you to worry about stuff that is never even going to happen.

For example, life expectancy in the United States has doubled during the twentieth century. We are better able to cure and control diseases than any other civilization in history.[6]

Yet, the media paints a different picture of our nation's health. In 1996, Bob Garfield, a magazine writer, reviewed articles about serious diseases published over the course of a year in the *Washington Post*, the *New York Times*, and *USA Today*. From his reading, he learned:

- Fifty-nine million Americans had heart disease.

- Fifty-three million suffered with migraines.

- Twenty-five million had osteoporosis.

- Sixteen million were obese.

- Three million had cancer.

- Ten million suffered from more obscure ailments such as temporomandibular joint disorders.

- Two million suffered brain injuries.[7]

Adding up the estimates, Garfield determined that most Americans are seriously sick. "Either as a society we are doomed, or someone is seriously double-dipping," he suggested.[8]

Don't listen to ABC, NBC, and "Woe Is Me" networks. They only try to create a culture of fear, making much ado about nothing. God does not want you to live in chronic fear because of what the media promote, often to sell their products.

I challenge you to use the Word of God as a powerful antidote for anxiety, fear, and panic attacks. Put on the armor of God that the apostle Paul describes, which includes the shield of faith to deflect the darts of the enemy. It also includes the sword of the Spirit, which is the Word of God (Eph. 6:17). Those divine fear fighter weapons give you supernatural power to defeat fear. They will release the power of God into every negative situation you face.

You have to decide to become a warrior and not a worrier. As a fear fighter, you can use the promises of the Word of God to overcome fear and worry.

In these days in which we are living, you are either going to be a warrior or a worrier. There will be no middle ground. When you hear bad economic news, are faced with a health crisis, or are tempted to worry about your children, choose to war against fear with God's Word instead of worrying and fearing the worst. When trouble comes, when tough times hit your life, refuse to cower in fear.

I don't understand why people have to go through stuff. I don't understand why cancer attacks good people who have never smoked a day in their lives, or why they must face the side effects of radiation and treatment. What do you do during these hard times? Either you give into fear and allow it to destroy your peace and well-being, or you become a warrior against it.

Being a warrior doesn't mean you don't ever feel afraid of the uncertainty of everything that could and might happen. But when fear threatens to engulf your mind, begin to declare as David did, "Whenever I am afraid, I will trust in You" (Ps. 56:3). In that place of declaring your faith, God will be very near to you.

COURAGE WITH COLD FEET

Do you know the story of Benaiah in the Old Testament? He was a hero during the reign of King David and became one of the king's mighty men. The Bible says that he killed a lion in a pit on a snowy day. He had the courage to jump down into a snowy pit with a lion and fight with him to the death. I call that courage with cold feet!

When we say we have cold feet, we mean we were afraid to do something. Courage is doing what you are afraid to do. It is not taking action without feeling any fear. Someone has said, "Courage is fear that has said its prayers."[9]

When you hear from God and He tells you to do something, you are filled with faith in that moment. It braces your spine like steel. You have heard from God! Then, when you move out in faith, you encounter the lion that is about to attack.

The apostle Peter tells us that we are in warfare with a lion: "Be sober, be vigilant; because your adversary the devil walks about like a roaring lion, seeking whom he may devour" (1 Pet. 5:8). That is when you get courage with cold feet. But it's all right. Mark Twain said, "Courage is resistance to fear, mastery of fear, not absence of fear; it is the mastery of fear."[10]

God needs some men and women in these troubled times to have the courage to say, "God said to do it, and I am going to do it!" Even if you have to get into knee-deep snow and fight a lion, you say, "Bring it on! I will not retreat in fear, because I know what God told me! I may have courage with cold feet, but the lion is not going to conquer me; I am going to conquer him!" The fact is, there is no real courage unless you are scared!

27

You may be at a point in your life right now where God has told you to do a hard thing. You know you have heard from God, and you are moving in faith. But you have started to feel the cold feet syndrome. Let me encourage you: be of good courage; the Lord is with you! Begin to declare, "Jesus is with me, and He has all power. I have faith for this!"

Unequal fights

If you are going to fight a lion, it would seem better to pick a warm sunshiny day rather than a cold snowy one. But we don't choose the timing of the fight—the enemy does—and it is an unequal fight. There is nothing equal about a lion and a man fighting. Obviously, the lion is stronger and has the advantage, but God is known for putting His people into unequal fights.

There is nothing equal about Jehoshaphat and his army marching into the flashing steel of the Syrian army with their praise team on the front line. He obviously never studied war strategy at West Point. It would give a five-star general a coronary arrest to think that he had to put musical instruments in his frontline army marching into enemy territory. What military officer would consider trying to defeat the enemy with a violin, harp, and tambourine?

There is nothing equal about the children of Israel marching around the impregnable walls of Jericho as a war strategy—or with David and his slingshot against the giant Goliath. But your "nothingness" plus God's "almightiness" equals giants falling down, walls falling down, armies ambushing themselves, and victory in every battle He gives you to fight. So be of good courage.

When you are facing insurmountable odds, that is the realm of courage. That is the place for courage with cold feet. I have been there, friend! When God told me to go to Gainesville to pastor Free Chapel, I went in courage with cold feet. When He said to build a church building, two and a half million dollars seemed like twenty-nine million dollars. Our congregation moved forward in courage with cold feet. Then when we bought more land for five million dollars, we had to summon courage to conquer our fear again. And when we began to build a sanctuary for seventeen million dollars, I said, "Here I am again, moving forward in courage with cold feet."

> ## FEAR FIGHTER
> God responds to courage
> that is demonstrated in the
> midst of fear.

But let me tell you what happens. When you get out there into the realm of the miraculous and have done all to stand in what God said, you begin to see miracles. Miracles happen in miracle territory. The Bible says, "Deep calls unto deep" (Ps. 42:7). When we began to launch out into the deep "waters," God already had people waiting to help us. People don't launch out for small needs. The big needs require the "deep waters."

Out of nowhere people began to send in donations to help pay for the "impossible" plan of God to reach many more souls. Some of these people had no prior involvement with the ministry, but they were moved by faith and wanted to be a part of what God had asked us to do.

God responds to courage that is demonstrated in the midst of fear. You can win your "unequal" battle when you decide to become a fear fighter.

COURAGE FOR YOUR PERSONAL STRUGGLES

Our family faced a very scary crisis with our oldest daughter when she went to my wife and told her that she had found a lump in her breast. My wife tells it as only a mother can:

> My grandmother died of breast cancer, and my mother was diagnosed with breast cancer many years ago. I will never forget the day my daughter, then seventeen, came to me and said that she found a lump in her breast. My heart filled with fear immediately, considering our family history. Trying not to scare her, I remained outwardly calm and told her it was probably nothing; girls have knots all the time. But inside I was panicking.
>
> The next day I took her to the doctor to check it out. The doctor found the lump and said it was the size of a quarter. Because of the breast cancer history, he sent us to Atlanta to a specialist and told us it didn't look good. We could not get in to see the specialist for a week, which was pure torture.
>
> That Wednesday night, we had a very powerful service. Our daughter, who was usually at the youth services on Wednesday nights, was in the sanctuary

that night singing with the praise team. The Spirit of God fell, and my husband felt prompted to call people forward for prayer.

She walked to the front weeping, along with many others who needed a touch from God that night. Later she said, "When I received prayer, something changed, and I felt the peace of God just engulf me. That terrible life-gripping fear left me."

When we got home, she came to us and said she couldn't find the lump. So we went back to our local doctor that next morning to see if he could find it. He couldn't.

As she lay on the examining table, I said, with concern, "It has to be there. Check again. Keep checking." But he said, "Whatever was there is not there now." So we returned to the specialist to have comprehensive tests done, and there was no lump to be found anywhere. The specialist said simply, "There is nothing there. We don't need to see you again until you are twenty."

In our crisis, we cried out to God for our daughter's health. We declared with cold-feet courage that God is her healer. We could have submitted to our fear and subjected her to surgery and other treatment. But God was there for us as we dared to call on Him in our scary crisis.

What will you do when you receive a bad report from your doctor, when you see the disease on your X-ray, or when you receive a pink slip from your employer? How will you react if you face foreclosure? Whether it is your marriage, your children, your finances, or your health that is in crisis, you have to decide whether to become a worrier or a warrior.

I wish every story ended with a miracle or healing, but it doesn't always happen that way. Sometimes God takes you through the fiery-furnace experience instead of delivering you from the fiery furnace.

In scary conditions, we can calm our fears and fill our hearts with courage to face life's challenges by focusing on God's Word.

You have to decide to take the Word of God and His promises, believing His great love for you, and go to war with those fear fighters. He will give you the courage if you choose to overcome your fear and fight for your victory, for your family's victory, and for whatever "unequal" fight the enemy has designed against you. Don't give in to much ado about nothing. Declare that you are a warrior, and say in the face of the lion, "It is written…" I encourage you to pray this prayer as you determine to be a victorious warrior:

Dear Jesus, forgive me for allowing my mind to be filled with irrational fear, for giving in to much ado about nothing. Help me to become a warrior instead of a worrier. I choose to obey Your commands and to go forward in courage even when I feel afraid. I say with David, "What time I am afraid, I will trust." I believe that I will begin to see miracles in my life as I take Your Word and believe Your promises, declaring in the face of the enemy, "It is written." Thank You, Lord. Amen.

FEAR FIGHTER'S ARSENAL

Much Ado About Nothing

Behold, God is my salvation, I will trust and not be afraid.

—Isaiah 12:2

Fear not, for I am with you;
Be not dismayed, for I am your God.
I will strengthen you,
Yes, I will help you,
I will uphold you with My righteous right hand.

—Isaiah 41:10

So shall My word be that goes forth from My mouth;
It shall not return to Me void,
But it shall accomplish what I please,
And it shall prosper in the thing for which I sent it.

—Isaiah 55:11

Do not be afraid of sudden terror,
Nor of trouble from the wicked when it comes;
For the Lord will be your confidence,
And will keep your foot from being caught.

—Proverbs 3:25–26

My Personal Fear Fighters

_____

_____

_____

_____

_____

_____

_____

_____

_____

_____

_____

_____

_____

_____

_____

_____

_____

My Fear Fighter Strategy

Have you begun to create a personal strategy for fighting fear?
What action steps will you take to become a fear fighter?

_____

_____

_____

_____

_____

_____

_____

_____

_____

_____

_____

_____

_____

_____

_____

_____

Moses's Song of Divine Safety

You who sit down in the High God's presence, spend
    the night in Shaddai's shadow,
Say this: "God, you're my refuge.
    I trust in you and I'm safe!"
That's right—he rescues you from hidden traps,
    shields you from deadly hazards.
His huge outstretched arms protect you—
    under them you're perfectly safe;
    his arms fend off all harm.
Fear nothing—not wild wolves in the night,
    not flying arrows in the day,
Not disease that prowls through the darkness,
    not disaster that erupts at high noon.
Even though others succumb all around,
    drop like flies right and left,
    no harm will even graze you.
You'll stand untouched, watch it all from a distance,
    watch the wicked turn into corpses.
Yes, because God's your refuge,
    the High God your very own home,
Evil can't get close to you,
    harm can't get through the door.
He ordered his angels
    to guard you wherever you go.
If you stumble, they'll catch you;
    their job is to keep you from falling.
You'll walk unharmed among lions and snakes,
    and kick young lions and serpents from the path.

"If you'll hold on to me for dear life," says God,
    "I'll get you out of any trouble.
I'll give you the best of care
    if you'll only get to know and trust me.
Call me and I'll answer, be at your side in bad times;
    I'll rescue you, then throw you a party.
I'll give you a long life,
    give you a long drink of salvation!"

—PSALM 91, THE MESSAGE

3

YOUR REFUGE FROM FEAR

WHERE DO YOU go when you need to feel safe? What do you do to get relief when you are facing threatening situations? Do you turn to food for comfort? Or alcohol? Or pills? Do you visit a psychiatrist? Or go to the mall for a shopping spree?

Many people suffer from terrible addictions they have developed to try to cope with their fears. Some become workaholics. Others are addicted to media of various kinds. Some escape into TV, becoming couch potatoes. Many spend hours every day on the Internet, Facebook, and Twitter. How do you escape the pressure and anxiety of your life?

Is coping with fear taking you into the world of escapism and addiction? If your answer is yes, I have good news for you. God has a safe place where you can live so that you don't have to be afraid. You don't have to escape into a dangerous addiction to get relief from your worry and fear. He wants to rescue you from every fear that torments your mind and emotions.

God wants to be your loving heavenly Father. He loves for His children to come running into His arms for comfort and protection. The Bible gives us beautiful pictures of this safe place. You know that David wrote many of the psalms, but one of the most beautiful psalms about our refuge from fear was written by Moses.

In Psalm 91, Moses describes your safe place of freedom from fear and all the attacks of the enemy against your life. He calls it the "shadow of the Almighty." In modern language, you could call it your very own home in God's presence. The good news is that when you run into God's shadow, He protects you from all harm with His great power. He wants you to know that you never have to live in fear again.

THE SHADOW OF THE ALMIGHTY

What is the shadow of the Almighty? The wilderness where Israel wandered for forty years was really an extremely hot desert. There was no shade there except what was provided by the tents in which the people lived. As a nomadic people, their only refuge from the burning sun was in the shadow of their tents. So they understood this powerful metaphor Moses used to describe their safe place in God—in the shadow of the Almighty.

To really appreciate what Moses was saying, you also need to understand the law of hospitality that God gave His people. It was a law that told them how to treat strangers who came into their camp.

FEAR FIGHTER

Christ will restore back to you
everything you lost as a result
of sin's power in your life.

If you were lost in the desert, were hungry, thirsty, or needed protection from an enemy, you could go into Israel's camp. The children of Israel were required to give you the help you needed because of the law of hospitality. The process was simple.

First, you had to find out the chief shepherd's name. Then, you would go and grab the cord on his tent and begin to cry out for his help. When you did that, the law of hospitality required him to take you in and help you. You could find safety in the shadow of his tent.

All of Israel understood that when they took someone into their dwelling, they had to protect them with their life. Do you remember when angels went to rescue Lot from God's judgment on Sodom? Lot invited the angels to come into his home. Then, the wicked men of the city came to Lot's home. They threatened to destroy it if he did not let the angels come out so they could abuse them. Instead of giving in to these men, Lot offered them his virgin daughters. (See Genesis 19.)

As a father of four precious daughters, I could not fathom Lot's offer to trade his daughters for the well-being of the guests in his home. How could he allow his daughters to be violated by these wicked men? But the law of hospitality required Lot to protect those angels with his life. He had invited them into his home, and he was responsible for their safety. Lot had to do all in his power to rescue them from harm.

In Moses's song, he shows this same divine hospitality of God that will rescue you from fear. When you come to His presence and call on His name, He will go to all extremes to protect you from all evil. God's name El Shaddai describes first of all His power (El) to protect you—He has all power! He has the power of a lion to devour its prey and defend you against every enemy.

Second, His name Shaddai describes His love and tenderness for you. It means "strong-breasted one," which refers to a gentle, tender, nursing mother. Sometimes you need the "El" of God's power to deliver you, and sometimes you just need His tenderness to hold you and comfort you. God says to you that He will be all that you need Him to be.

There have been times in my life when I did not need the lion strength or the thundering power of God. I felt so vulnerable, so weary, so tested and tried. I needed the gentleness of my Shaddai to hold me.

If I had not received His tenderness, nourishment, and strength as He comforted me in those painful trials, I would have given up. But my El Shaddai was there in that secret place to grant me

His blessing and favor. All I had to do was call on His name and pull the cord of His tent.

CHRIST, OUR CHIEF SHEPHERD

Do you remember the woman with the issue of blood? She believed that if she could just touch the hem of Jesus's garment, she would be healed. What was that hem? It was the cord of the tent. She ran to Jesus to seek the healing she needed. When she touched His garment, Jesus knew someone had pulled on that cord. Immediately, He turned to see who had touched Him.

The disciples were disgusted. They pointed out that with so many people in the crowd around Him, everyone was touching Him. But Jesus knew the difference between the jostling crowd and the touch of a woman who had run into His shadow. She had sought to touch Him with one purpose—the cry in her heart for His divine help. Jesus recognized her faith and pronounced her healed of her twelve-year sickness.

Do you need to be rescued from fear? From sickness? From financial problems? With tender love, Jesus will answer your cry for help. All of His power is at your disposal when you run into His shadow. You can have all the promises Moses described in his song—in the name of Jesus. In Christ's shadow is healing and health, blessing and favor—and protection from all evil.

YOUR CITY OF REFUGE

God told Joshua to build six cities of refuge as safe places for the guilty to run into. According to the Law, it was legal for a family member to try to kill you to get justice for the person you killed.

But when you killed someone accidentally, you could run to a city of refuge to hide. (See Joshua 20.)

When the leaders of the city were told what had happened, they were required to protect you from the vengeance of your enemy. The only stipulation was that you never leave that city of refuge until the high priest died. When that happened, you were free to go back to your family and take everything back you had lost because of your guilt.

Jesus Christ is called the High Priest of our confession (Heb. 3:1). When you run to Him to seek refuge, He asks you to confess what you have done. Then He offers you forgiveness and gives you His protection. He has paid for your pardon by taking all of your guilt to the cross of Calvary. He has set you free from everything your past says has a right to destroy you, judge you, and condemn you.

> ## FEAR FIGHTER
>
> With God, there are no boundaries, just possibilities.

Christ will restore back to you everything you lost as a result of sin's power in your life. He is your High Priest. You can enter into a covenant of blessing on your life when you call on His name. As you learn to dwell in Christ, you can live a life free from the destructive power of fear and sin.

Of course, God never promised you a life without problems.

You cannot avoid the attacks of the enemy against your life. You need to understand how to conquer his threats. There are three kinds of attacks the enemy uses to threaten your family and you:

- The *expected* attack
- The *unexpected* attack
- The *unfounded* attack

THE EXPECTED ATTACK

In Moses's song, he describes God's protection for you against the lion. The lion represents the threat of *expected* attacks against your life and family. When you are in the presence of a lion, you expect to be attacked. There are no surprises here. Life comes complete with built-in problems.

Are you facing relationship problems in your family, problems in your finances, your health, or your ministry? Then you need to receive God's divine protection from that expected attack of the lion.

The Bible refers to Satan as a roaring lion: "Be sober, be vigilant; because your adversary the devil walks about like a roaring lion, seeking whom he may devour" (1 Pet. 5:8). As a believer, you can expect that attacks of the enemy will come, no matter who you are. You should not be amazed—or afraid—when you are attacked because the Bible says it will happen.

Instead of giving in to fear, you have to stand up and call on the name of the Lord. He has promised to protect you when you do. Take a stand against the lion's plan for destruction. "Resist him, steadfast in the faith" (v. 9). When our daughter faced the threat of the lion against her body, we prayed. We called on El Shaddai. He heard our cry and rescued her from that potentially life-threatening disease.

You don't have to fear the expected attack of the lion. God has promised you supernatural victory over every threat of the enemy. Run to His shadow, and use His wonderful name as the fear fighter you need to overcome the enemy's expected attacks.

THE UNEXPECTED ATTACK

Moses declared that God would protect you from snakes. An adder lies quietly under a rock or behind a bush and strikes when you least expect it. It represents the *unexpected* attack from the enemy. When you are attacked by an adder, you say things like, "Wow, I didn't see that coming!"—that accident, that job loss, that relational problem. "The adder was just lying there under that rock, and I did not see it coming to attack."

You know how frightening that unexpected attack can be. Somehow, the element of surprise takes you off guard. You feel overwhelming fear in that moment. But you don't have to freak out when the adder attacks unexpectedly. Run into the shadow of El Shaddai. You need to know that miracles can strike as suddenly as tragedies! Just call on the name of the Lord!

Do what the apostle Paul did when the deadly snake grabbed his wrist, and shake it off into the fire. (See Acts 28.) When an adder attack of the enemy strikes you, don't just let it chew on you; shake it off!

If the adder tries to chew on your mind, filling it with fear, resentment, anger, or unforgiveness, shake it off. Don't allow him to gain advantage over you by listening to his sneaky accusations. The devil will try to steal your peace and joy, your relationships, and your faith in God. He will try to strike your children, your finances, and your future.

Run to the tent of El Shaddai, and allow Him to cleanse your heart from the chewing adder. He will destroy the traumatic effects of the unexpected attack on your life. God will restore to you all the enemy has tried to steal from you.

Satan is a joy robber. His unexpected attacks can chew away your joy. He wants you to get up every morning and hate your life. It can happen to any of us. Depression is always looming over us, but you don't have to take it. Just declare, "The Lord is my refuge. The Lord is my life. The Lord is my safe place." The Bible says that at His right hand there are pleasures forevermore (Ps. 16:11). God wants you to be a happy, carefree child living in His presence.

Satan wants to steal your peace. I prayed with a person who was being tormented by demon spirits. They kept him from sleeping at night, robbing him of his peace. I told him there is only one place where you can be safe.

You can go to a psychiatrist, but they can't make you safe. You can try to get relief with medication or alcohol, but you will only find the true place of safety in the shadow of El Shaddai, in Christ Jesus our Lord.

I know what it is to be attacked by devils. I have seen them with my eyes. But that is when I run to El Shaddai. I pull on His tent cord and call on His name. In that place of divine safety, all the armies and angels of heaven step up and declare, "He's under the shadow of the Almighty! We have to rescue him!"

THE UNFOUNDED ATTACK

Moses also described God's protection for you from the fear of the dragon (Ps. 91:13, KJV). The dragon, in the original Hebrew language, referred to a marine or land monster, a whale, or a serpentine creature.

When I was a boy in school, I looked at maps of the early civilization that had pictures of dragons on them. The seamen who explored the world would not go to the places where the dragons were located. They were afraid to go beyond a certain point that had not been explored for fear of being devoured by a sea monster.

That is the way the devil tries to intimidate you. He keeps you from going beyond a certain point in your walk with God through fear of the unknown. Don't dream beyond this point. Don't reach for anything more, because the dragon will devour you. He hisses at you to keep you from pursuing your dream. But with God, there are no boundaries, just possibilities.

Because the children of Israel were in the middle of a desert, it seems highly improbable that they would have to face a dragon. Nevertheless, God wanted them to know they were protected from such a threatening beast.

This unlikely threat from the dragon represents your *unfounded* fears of attack. However remote the possibility of this attack, the enemy's threat can make you cower in your mind. You suffer the same pangs of worry and fear as though it will happen.

Unfounded attacks. Unfounded fears. You quiver inside and say, "I just know it's coming. I have been doing pretty good for a while, but I remember my daddy. He did OK for a while, and then he just kept messing up. I might be just like him."

Satan tries to plant all kinds of unfounded fear and worry in your mind over things that are highly improbable. He will tell you that you are going to lose it all, that your children are going to hell, or that you have cancer somewhere in your body. His goal is to make you cower before an unfounded fear. But God's power is greater than Satan's unfounded fears.

Do you remember how many of your worries are valid? Only 8 percent are even likely to happen. Most worry and fear is really much ado about nothing. Yet, Satan is a master of painting pictures of impending disaster.

> FEAR FIGHTER
>
> "He's under the shadow of the Almighty! We have to rescue him!"

You see a plane crash on the evening television news, and you are scheduled to fly the next day. Your heart begins to pound, and you consider canceling your flight. Or a relative has a heart attack, and suddenly you feel like your heart is beating strangely. You need to change that devilish picture in your mind and run into the safety you have in Christ's shadow.

Your unfounded fears may involve your personal relationships. You hear someone's conversation or think about the way they looked at you and the devil will make you think everyone in the room is talking about you. Lighten up a little. You are not that important to everybody. (Speaking for myself, I don't meditate on any of my congregation's responses too long. If I did, I could have fifteen or twenty hits coming at me at the same time.) That is the dragon of fear painting unfounded pictures of disaster in your head.

You have to yell back at him with the truth of the Scriptures. Tell the devil you know that God loves you, no matter what people think of you. Declare to him that you are not going to fail. Use your fear fighters from the Word of God, and declare that you are being "transformed...from glory to glory" (2 Cor. 3:18). Tell the enemy that the Lord is the author and the finisher of your faith (Heb. 12:2). He is your El Shaddai!

God did not promise you that you would never have any problems. But when problems come, He wants you to know that you never have to be afraid. No fear can exist in His love when you dwell under His shadow.

God wants you to know that when you enter the protection of His shadow, He will go to all extremes to take care of you. It doesn't matter if you are dealing with the expected attack of the lion or the unexpected attack of the adder. It doesn't matter if you are facing fear of the unfounded attack of a dragon. Just call on the name of the Lord, and He will rescue you.

LIVING IN THE SHADOW OF SAFETY

We live in a world where there are threats of financial loss, random shootings, and child abduction. Divorce, drug addiction, cancer, atheistic new age philosophies, nuclear destruction, and many other forms of evil taunt our lives.

It is not enough just to *visit* the shadow of God when you are in trouble. You have to make God's presence your very own home. The key to Moses's song is learning to dwell in the secret place, to abide under the shadow of the Almighty. To escape from the enemy's attacks, you need to follow biblical principles for living continually in the safety of God's shadow.

Confession

I tell my congregation often that "devil talk" will bring the devil on the scene, and "God talk" will bring God on the scene. There will always be things trying to attack you to pull you out of God's presence, out from under His shadow. But confessing the truth of the Word of God will keep you from giving into the enemy's lies.

> ## FEAR FIGHTER
>
> "In Him we live and move and have our being."

When you speak victory, you release the power of God for victory. When you speak defeat, that is what you will get. To live in the presence of God you have to confess the power of God to protect you and your family. You have to get some tent pegs from God's Word to drive into your mind and keep you speaking the truth. Declare the promises of God for your life.

Worship

The apostle Paul declared of Christ, "In Him we live and move and have our being" (Acts 17:28). God wants you to live in constant communion with Him. That is how you receive His constant provision and protection.

You cultivate communion by learning to worship God in spirit and in truth. Praising God and thanking Him for His love and provision keeps you dependent on Him. You need to recognize that He is your source of life. That will keep you seeking Him and living under His shadow.

Moses did not have very peaceful circumstances in his life. He led over two million people for forty years through the wilderness. The Bible says that the people complained and rebelled against him. At times they wanted to return to Egypt or get rid of Moses. Yet, Moses is called the meekest man who ever lived.

How did he do it? He had learned to dwell in the presence of God. When he entered the tent to commune with God, all the people stood at their tent doors to see what God would do. They knew that he had learned to commune with God and to hear His voice.

The enemy knows whether you dwell in the shadow or just visit there when you are in trouble. He knows that his attacks are not successful when you are dwelling in the safety of God's presence. Your communion with God will keep you there.

Become a shadow on location.

When God pours His life into you, refreshes and blesses you, He has a greater purpose than just your own welfare. He wants you to become a shadow on location for someone else's desert experience. He will allow people to start pulling on the cord of your tent. Then He expects you to open your heart to them and pour into them the truth you have received.

God wants you to share with others the freedom you have found in Christ. He will help you to lead them to Christ and to teach them how to dwell in His shadow. You will know the joy of seeing their lives set free from fear and the destructions of the enemy.

As Paul and Silas praised God at midnight in prison, God sent an earthquake that opened their prison doors. Yet, they did not run away as free men. They stayed there and told the prisoners and the jailer about the wonderful freedom in Christ they had found. They led the jailer and his household to Christ.

You have to remember that you get delivered to bring deliverance to others! God wants to pour His life and power through you. He will use you to become a shadow on location to rescue your family, friends, and other precious lives from destruction.

FEAR FIGHTER

Tell the enemy that the Lord is the author and the finisher of your faith.

I encourage you to learn to dwell under the shadow of the Almighty. Let your heart respond to the love of God, who wants to rescue you and keep you safe. Your responsibility is to call on His name and ask Him for His divine help.

Dear Lord Jesus, thank You for the safe place You have provided for me through Your death on Calvary and Your resurrection. Jesus, I call on Your name right now to help me. I surrender my life to Your care. Let me know You as my El Shaddai. Please become my shadow of the Almighty, my divine place of safety from evil. Teach me to live there in constant fellowship and communion with You. Then, I ask You to make me a shadow on location to others who need to find a safe place in You. Thank You, Jesus. Amen.

FEAR FIGHTER'S ARSENAL

Your Refuge From Fear

The Lord is my rock and my fortress and my deliverer…
My stronghold and my refuge.

—2 Samuel 22:2–3

I will call upon the Lord, who is worthy to be praised;
So shall I be saved from my enemies.

—Psalm 18:3

Call upon Me in the day of trouble;
I will deliver you, and you shall glorify Me.

—Psalm 50:15

For You have been a shelter for me,
A strong tower from the enemy.

—Psalm 61:3

And He led them on safely,
So that they did not fear.

—Psalm 78:53

My Personal Fear Fighters

_____

_____

_____

_____

_____

_____

_____

_____

_____

_____

_____

_____

_____

_____

_____

_____

_____

4

YOUR FIGHT OF FAITH

FROM YOUR PLACE of safety in the shadow of the Almighty, you need to know how to win over fear by fighting the good fight of faith. In faith, you called on the name of the Lord, and He rescued you. Now, you have to take responsibility to let your faith in God grow to conquer fear and live in victory in every situation you face in life.

Your faith in God's protection and provision is a powerful fear fighter to deliver you from the enemy's attacks. Fear activates Satan's work in your life. In that same way, faith activates God's work in your life. Simply put, faith attracts God as fear attracts Satan. Fear becomes a conduit for Satan's destruction in your life. Faith is the conduit through which God's supernatural power flows into your life.

Jesus referred to the devil as a thief who comes to "steal, and to kill, and to destroy" (John 10:10). And Jesus referred to Himself as the One who comes to give life abundantly. So, when you release your faith, you are releasing the abundant life of God into your situation.

The Bible tells us to fight the good fight of faith (1 Tim. 6:12). It is not always easy to be filled with faith when fear is trying to attack you. Are you in a faith fight for your future, your marriage, or your finances? Then you know that unless you win the fight of faith, what you fear can become a reality, which can defeat you in your walk with God.

In order to win your faith fight, you will have to overcome what your five senses are telling you. Your mind and emotions are tied to your five senses, and fear attacks you through what they tell you. You must not allow yourself to be driven by the fear that tries to rule your five senses. You have to engage in a faith fight based on God's truth in spite of what your senses tell you.

Do what you see and hear rule your life? Determine your decisions? Control your feelings? Then you need to conquer these "kings" through faith in order to receive the promises of God for your life.

CONQUERING YOUR FIVE KINGS

Joshua led the children of Israel into battle against five kings who were trying to make war against them in the Promised Land. These five kings were determined to defeat Israel and rob them of their inheritance. God was with Joshua and the people, and He helped them defeat these armies.

But the five kings ran away and hid themselves in a cave, fearing for their lives. When they were discovered, Joshua told his warriors to bring the five kings out of the dark cave. Then he told his captains to put their feet on the necks of those kings. He said, "Do not be afraid, nor be dismayed; be strong and of good courage, for thus the LORD will do to all your enemies against whom you fight" (Josh. 10:25).

Did you know that your five senses are your enemies? Just as Joshua's captains may have been dismayed by those five kings who wanted to rule Israel, you will end up being dismayed if you allow your senses to rule your life. To be dismayed means "to be torn apart" or "to fall apart." The devil wants to tear your mind apart and rob you of peace. He wants to tear your emotions apart and give you a nervous breakdown. He works to tear your family apart. The good news is that you don't have to be dismayed; God doesn't want you to fall apart

First, Joshua commanded his captains to bring those kings out of the dark cave where they were hiding. Then, they had to put their feet on the necks of those enemies. They had to confront them, subdue them. They were declaring to them, "You will not rule over our lives!"

I believe these five kings represent the faith fight we are in today. They represent what we see, hear, smell, taste, and touch in the natural world. We use our five senses to determine what is going on in the world around us. God gave them to us for that purpose. But they become tyrants of fear if we believe everything they tell us and allow them to rule our lives.

When you hear a bad report from a doctor, don't let what you hear put fear into your heart. When you see the economy tanking, don't let what you see rob you of your faith in God's provision. When you feel bad, don't let Satan tell you that you have cancer. You have to refuse to let your fives senses rule as kings in your mind and heart.

Joshua was telling his captains not to be dismayed. Don't fall apart when these five kings show up in your life. Put your foot on their necks and subdue them. You have to determine from this day forward to overcome the five kings of your senses in order to live in victory over fear. You need to let your faith rule in your mind and heart. Your faith has to rule over your senses in every life situation.

Thank God for faith that works as a sixth sense in every person who is a believer in Jesus Christ! The Bible says we walk by faith, not by sight (2 Cor. 5:7). Faith is our sixth sense, and it says, "In spite of what I see, in spite of what I am hearing, in spite of what I am feeling, or what I can taste or smell, I believe everything is going to be all right. I am tuned in to another sense!"

It is this faith sense that lets me know I don't have to live my life in fear and disarray. I don't have to be dismayed in life because of what my senses tell me. God will give me victory over my senses when the enemy tries to fill them with fear. I can put their "necks" under my feet and walk by faith, declaring God's victory in that fearful situation.

Your five senses are faith killers. Unless you put these "kings" under your feet, the enemy will steal your promise, your dream, and everything God has given you. You are to be purpose driven, not fear driven. You are not to be driven by emotions based on what your senses tell you. If you let your senses rule, you will be one defeated, schizophrenic, messed-up person—up one minute, down the next!

Your faith fight will require that you learn to keep your foot on the neck of your five senses.

WHAT DO YOU SMELL?

Do you remember when the three Hebrew boys were thrown into the furnace because they would not bow down to worship an idol? (See Daniel 3.) They declared that their God was able to deliver them from that death sentence. But even if He didn't, they would not worship another god.

The king demanded that the furnace be heated seven times hotter because of their insolence. It was so hot that the men who threw them into it died immediately. Those God-fearing young men had to go through that fiery ordeal. There was no escape from it.

Sometimes God will allow you to go through a trial instead of sparing you from it. But your faith in God will allow Him to deliver you out of it. Either He will deliver you from having to go through it or He will deliver you out of it! Walking in faith is a win-win situation!

What amazed me is that when these Hebrew boys were thrown into the furnace, they were bound. Yet, when the king looked into the furnace, he saw four men walking around, loosed from their bondages. They were set free from the ropes that bound them. Apparently, the only thing that deadly fire could touch was their bondages!

The Scriptures say that when the king ordered the three Hebrews to come out of the furnace, the fire had no power on their bodies. The hair of their head was not singed, and *there was not even a smell of smoke on them*. Even though they walked through a fiery furnace, they did not smell like what they had gone through.

The aroma of praise

No matter how hot the fire you have to walk through, or how difficult the trial, you don't have to *smell* like what you have come through. Some people go through divorce, and twenty years later they still *smell* like it. Others go through a bad business deal, and years later they are still whining and depressed over it. You have to get the victory over the smell of your circumstances. You don't have to live like you have walked through fire.

> ## FEAR FIGHTER
>
> Walking in faith is a win-win situation!

Some people remind me of the grandfather whose grandchildren rubbed Limburger cheese into his mustache while he slept.

When he got up, he took a deep breath and said, "Shoo! This bedroom stinks!" He went down to breakfast and took another deep breath and said, "Shoo! This kitchen stinks!" When he went into the backyard and took a whiff, he said, "Shoo! The whole world stinks!"

Do you know that your attitude can smell of negativism and defeat so that you feel like everything stinks? You need to lift your eyes to God and get cleansed of the Limburger cheese effects. Declare in faith that God is with you and that you will make it through your fiery trial, without even the smell of smoke clinging to you.

What really happens in the fiery trial is that your bondages are burned off. When God delivers you in the fire, you are set free to raise your hands and praise God. You need to let the aroma of praise be like incense in your life, a sacrifice to the living God. You can live in greater freedom and rejoicing because of what you have been delivered from in the fiery trial.

The Bible says that when God smelled the burning flesh of the animals sacrificed on the altar, it was like a sweet aroma to Him (Lev. 2:2). When you place your carnal nature on the altar, refusing to allow your senses to rule your life, God says it is a sweet aroma to Him. You might say, "That stinks! I hate my life right now!" But God loves the aroma of your carnal nature being sacrificed to Him. It allows His life to reign in you. He loves seeing you decrease so that He can increase His victory through faith in your heart. God wants to smell the aroma of praise from your lips because of His deliverance in your life.

Victory over the smell of death

When Lazarus died, Jesus did not appear on the scene until four days later. When He told Mary and Martha to have the stone over his tomb rolled away, they protested. They told Jesus that he would already be stinking from the smell of death. Before Jesus could get victory into that situation for that family, He had to put His foot on the neck of the king of smell.

They had seen Jesus do miracles and even raise the dead, but they had not seen Him work in the arena of "stink." They were convinced that it was too late for His intervention. You may feel that your situation stinks and that it is too late for help. You have to put your foot on that king of smell that tells you it's over.

You may feel your marriage stinks, your finances stink, or your health stinks. Maybe you have been through a fiery situation and you still "smell" like what you have been through. Jesus said to them that if they could just believe Him, He would give them a resurrection miracle like they had not seen.

Faith is not determined by how long or who says it is too late. God is the God of resurrection! He is able to make dead things live again, no matter how great the "stink." If you can just get your foot on the neck of that king who "smells" so bad and believe God, your miracle is on the way.

Just declare, "It's never too late for faith." Begin to praise God for what He is going to do. The smell of smoke doesn't have to cling to you for the rest of your life. What you went through doesn't have to define your present or your tomorrow. God can deliver you even from the smell of death!

What Do Your Feelings Tell You?

Do you remember the story of Isaac blessing his sons when he had become blind and was nearing his death? (See Genesis 27.) When Jacob, the younger son, wanted to steal his older brother's birthright, his mother helped him to disguise himself as Esau. Esau was a hairy man, and Jacob had smooth skin. So Rebekah wrapped Jacob's hands in goat's hair and brought Esau's clothes for him to wear.

Jacob went to his father, pretending to be Esau. Isaac asked him to come near so that he could feel him. Then Isaac told him that he sounded like Jacob but he felt like Esau. But Isaac decided that he would trust what he felt instead of what he heard in the sound of Jacob's voice.

It matters what you hear. The Bible says that faith comes by hearing the Word of God (Rom. 10:17). When you hear the truth, you need to believe it. But Isaac decided to trust what he felt over what he heard. He made the wrong decision and gave the birthright destined for the firstborn to his second son. He was deceived by what he felt.

FEAR FIGHTER

It's never too late for faith.

Has anyone ever told you, "Don't be so touchy"? That phrase describes the fallacy of your feelings that misunderstand and react selfishly to situations. Of course, your sense of touch is useful for your natural life, but your feelings that reside in your emotions must not be allowed to rule your life. You cannot trust these feelings apart from faith. They do not always respond according to truth and can deceive you.

"Well, Pastor, I got my feelings hurt, so I haven't spoken to my family in over a year." Get over it! Learn to forgive. Refuse to be offended. Practice love! Put your foot on the neck of your feelings that are robbing you of relationships.

If you let feelings rule your life, they will mess you up. This king will defeat you! "Well, I just don't feel God anymore." It doesn't matter what you feel. Victory is not a feeling; it is a fact of faith. Faith is more powerful than your feelings. Sometimes I feel saved, and sometimes I don't. But I am saved by faith, not by feelings.

Have you ever thought of Noah's ark and the year of confinement those eight people had with all those animals? You don't read of fights among the animals or the people. They knew they were in a powerful storm, surviving on the same boat, and they had to get along with each other. They must have had all kinds of feelings in those unnatural surroundings, but they did not dare allow them to mess them up.

When you are in a stormy trial, don't allow the enemy to get your feelings riled up. The storm we face in the world today makes it important for us to stay in the ark of safety. As members of the body of Christ in the church, we don't need to be growling at each other and getting our feelings hurt. Your petty little feelings can cause you to miss out on God's plan for your life.

I think the last thing God told Noah when He shut the door

on the ark was to be sure to keep the woodpeckers above the water line. Because in every ark—church—there are a few woodpeckers that want to get below the water line and sink the whole ship. They get their feelings hurt over what someone said. Or they want a position. Or they have an opinion, and if it doesn't go their way, they want to bring it all down.

Don't be a woodpecker that allows your feelings to hurt others. Don't give in to your feelings; give in to faith. Conquer the king of feelings by exercising your faith in God's Word.

Do You Believe What You See?

Have you been defeated because of what you saw with your eyes? Has the promise of God been aborted because you chose to believe what you saw instead of what God had promised? You can get it back if you will refuse to believe what your senses tell you and walk by faith in God's promises.

Sight is a powerful "king" that rules through your senses. When Jacob was an old man and his sons brought to him the many-colored coat of Joseph, he believed what his eyes told him. The brothers had sold Joseph to get rid of him. But they dipped Joseph's coat in goat's blood so that it looked like Joseph had been attacked by a wild beast.

Jacob saw that bloody coat and declared that an evil beast had devoured his son. That was the picture that the jealous brothers of Joseph had painted for their grief-stricken father. He said, "Without doubt Joseph is torn to pieces" (Gen. 37:33).

Without doubt means believing with perfect faith. But it was not true, even though it was totally believable to Jacob's eyes.

His experience shows that it is possible to have perfect faith in a lie. Jacob imagined the fate of his son based on the evidence he saw with his eyes. He did not know that what he was seeing was a lie.

In reality, Joseph was alive, and he would sit in an exalted position in Egypt, which would allow him to prepare wagonloads of food to send to his family for their survival. But his father lived all those years in grief because he had put perfect faith in a lie.

Do you have more faith in a lie than you do in the truth? You saw the X-ray and decided to believe what you and the doctor are seeing. You have to decide if you will believe what the doctor says or declare the Word of God in faith. Maybe you lost your job and the economy is getting worse. Will you believe the financial circumstances you see, or will you put your faith in the God who promises to supply all you need?

When Elisha the prophet was being pursued by a great army of horses and chariots, his servant saw the multitude and cried out in dismay, "What shall we do?" (2 Kings 6:15). Elisha told his servant not to be afraid. Then he asked the Lord to open the servant's eyes to see what he saw, and the young man saw the mountains filled with horses and chariots of fire around Elisha. The angels of the Lord were coming to defend them against the enemy, and they had the enemy surrounded!

If you just look at ground level, you will miss the miraculous. God doesn't want your feelings falling apart because of what you see all around you. He wants you to look to Him and to know that, in your darkest moment, you don't have to be afraid. You can be assured that your help comes from the Lord.

You may not be seeing anything encouraging right now. But

don't just look at the problems; look at God's promises! Don't just see the enemy; see God's angels! Don't just consider the difficulties; consider the Lord! Put your foot on the neck of what you are seeing, and declare, "I will live by faith and not by sight!"

Jesus told us that when the last days come, we will see terrible things come on the earth. We will see wars and rumors of wars and all kinds of natural disasters like we are seeing now. But He said that instead of fearing the world's dilemmas, that is the time to look up because your redemption is very near. These world problems are just signs for us to look up and to see the Word of the Lord coming to pass.

Don't let what you see with your natural eyes deceive you. Did you hear about the little boy who got a new white football for Christmas? He was kicking it in his yard, and it accidentally went into his neighbor's yard. His neighbor had a hen house. When the rooster saw the big white football roll into his chicken coop, he called all the hens out to see it. He said, "Come on, gals. You need to get with it. I don't mean to complain, but this is what they're putting out next door!"

You just can't always trust what your eyes see. You could be putting perfect faith in a lie. Let your faith tell you what you are supposed to see.

WHAT HAVE YOU HEARD?

In your faith fight, you are also going to have to put your foot on the neck of what you hear. I promise you that you will hear a lot of discouraging words and accusations. The enemy will whisper to you to quit, to give up because you can't make it anyway. He will speak fear to you: "You are going bankrupt. You are going to die. No one loves you." You cannot allow what you hear to rob you of your faith.

Elijah had announced the word of the Lord to King Ahab that no rain would fall for years (1 Kings 17:1). After three years without rain, everyone was talking about famine and wondering how they were going to survive. They were hearing animals dying and people moaning in hunger.

But Elijah was hearing the sound of abundance of rain. He was tuned in to hearing the voice of the Lord once again. Elijah was saying, "I've got a sixth sense. I've got my foot on the neck of what everyone else is hearing. I am hearing something else in the Spirit. I hear the sound of abundance."

When the economy goes south and everyone is hearing recession, bankruptcy, and foreclosure, what are you hearing? What are you tuned in to? You need to tune out fear and tune in to the voice of the Lord for your provision.

Elijah heard God's voice for his own supernatural provision during that famine. You have to decide if you are going to hear the sound of disease, dying, and defeat. Or are you going to hear the sound of health, life, and victory? Will you trust what you hear in the natural, or will you tune your spiritual ear of faith to hear God's promises?

You will never hear from God's Word that you are not going to make it. You will never hear that God is not faithful or that He does not care. The Bible teaches that in spite of what you are hearing around you, faith will believe God's faithfulness and fight for your victory! You have to put your foot on the neck of what you have been listening to that is contrary to God's Word.

When Jesus was praying for the Father to glorify His name, God the Father spoke to Him from heaven. He said, "I have both glorified it and will glorify it again" (John 12:28). Some people standing around heard Him and thought it was thunder. They could not recognize the voice of God; it sounded like a loud noise to their ears. Isn't that amazing? Someone can hear the Word of God, and another standing right beside them can hear only a bunch of racket.

What you hear is important. You have to decide to put your foot on the neck of the racket you hear and listen for the word of the Lord over your life. Don't listen to suggestions of defeat. Begin to hear the promise of the Father for you that your dream is going to live! All you have to do is put your doubtful hearing under your feet.

WHAT DO YOU TASTE?

Do you remember the story of Elisha during a time of famine in the land of Gilgal? (See 2 Kings 4.) He told his servant to make a stew for the sons of the prophets who were starving. So they went to gather wild herbs and gourds to make a pot of stew. But when they were eating it, they cried out to the prophet that there was death in the pot. They tasted poison in it and were going to throw it away.

Elisha had a better remedy. He told them to bring him some meal, which represents the Word of God, and mix it into the pot of stew. The Bible says they ate the stew, and there was no harm in it.

What do you "taste"? Do you taste the fear that your family will fall apart? Or the fear of death? Sometimes, the taste of bitterness in life's disappointments is like poison to us. What will you do when offense, unforgiveness, and bitterness threaten your marriage? Will you throw it away to get rid of the poison?

The Word of God has the answer to the taste of poison that attacks your life. He gives grace to forgive, to heal offense, and to remove bitterness from the most difficult situation. You have to put it under your feet by faith.

In order to overcome this king of taste in your soul, you have to learn to forgive others. If you allow bitterness to have a place in your life because people have slandered your character or criticized your family, it will destroy you. Some of you have to forgive God for situations that you do not understand. And some of you have to forgive yourselves for regrets and failures in your life.

Don't let the bitter trials of life leave a bad taste in your mouth. The Bible says, "O taste and see that the LORD is good; blessed is the man who trusts in Him!" (Ps. 34:8).

God wants to give you victory over your senses. If you are ruled by your senses, you will live a life of torment. But faith is greater than those five kings. As your sixth sense, it will triumph over every lie your senses try to get you to believe. Often, they are lurking in the darkness convincing you of their power. You have to pull them out into the light, put your foot on their necks, and refuse to allow them to rule.

What are you facing? What are you hearing? What are you seeing? What are you feeling? God is greater than your worst fear or nightmare. You just have to let the sixth sense of faith operate in your life.

Your senses will cause you to live in fear. If you believe only what you see, hear, feel, smell, or taste in the natural realm of your soul, you will miss the spiritual reality that faith wants to give you. God wants you to know He loves you. He knows everything about you, and in spite of it, He is for you!

Though others may see trash, God sees treasure in you. That's what He saw in me when nobody else did. When I didn't even see it in myself, He saw treasure. Let your faith see what God sees in you. Don't trust what you see and hear and feel about yourself.

Fight the fight of faith. Take authority over the natural realm of the senses. When you agree with the Word of God instead of your senses, you will be victorious in life. You will walk in a realm of miracles you did not know was possible. Your dream will live if you let faith fight for you!

Your Faith Will Fight for You!

Faith knows how to win. Faith has never lost a battle. If you don't believe that, ask Moses, who faced the Red Sea. Ask David, who ran from Saul for his life. Ask Daniel, who was thrown into the lion's den. Your faith is a divine weapon that will defeat every attack of the enemy. It will swallow up fear and let you walk in the purposes of God.

David declared that he could run through a troop and leap over a wall through His faith in God (2 Sam. 22:30). I have learned that for every miracle God gives me, I first have to leap over the wall of my own self-imposed limitations that scream, "You can't do that!"

But if I make the leap, it is just a matter of time before God enables me to run against the troop and win the victory. Whether it is expansion in the ministry or a challenge with my family, my faith will fight for me. And your faith will fight for you!

[

FEAR FIGHTER

Faith has never lost a battle.

]

You have to expose those thoughts you hear in your mind that say, "It's no use. It's hopeless." Bring them out into the light, and see them through the eyes of faith for what they are. They form the wall that you must leap over in faith to receive God's miracle.

Faith fights fear—and wins!

As a believer, your faith in God fights against fear like the white blood cells fight against infection in your body. They destroy the infection and unwanted cause of disease. This is what happens when fear attacks and you declare the Word of God in faith:

"Faith, where are you going?"

"I'm going to fight for the believer who is being attacked by fear. He is calling on God, and my assignment is to eradicate the source of his fear!"

The Bible says that the fear of the Lord is clean (Ps. 19:9). Any other fear is dirty and has torment. Walking in the fear of the Lord is faith in action. It releases us from fear of the future, from fear of failure and every tormenting fear. Your faith will fight every fear, and it will always win!

Faith fights feelings—and wins!

You don't have to be ruled by negative feelings. In fact, not one of the "kings" of your five senses is a match for the power of faith released in your life. Faith praises God for the answer before it comes. It steps on the neck of every lie that opposes the purposes of God for your life. Faith can move mountains and always does the will of God in you and for you.

I encourage you to pray with me to allow faith—your sixth sense—to destroy the power of those five "kings" over your life:

> *In the name of Jesus, I come to You, Lord, and ask You to let the blood of Jesus cleanse me from the old "smoke" I have carried around from what I have been through. Help me to put my foot on the neck of all five senses that see and hear lies and believe them to be true. Help me to destroy the feelings that make me doubt Your promises. Remove the bitter taste of hurts, offenses, and unforgiveness in my heart. I put my foot on the neck of every king that tries to stop God's purpose in my life. I will fight the fight of faith and win the victory. Thank You, Lord. In Jesus's name, amen.*

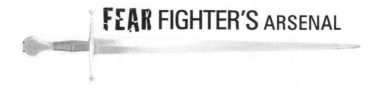

FEAR FIGHTER'S ARSENAL

Your Fight of Faith

Through God we shall do valiantly;
For He it is that shall tread down our enemies.

—Psalm 60:12

Yet in all these things we are more than conquerors through Him who loved us.

—Romans 8:37

Thanks be to God, who gives us the victory through our Lord Jesus Christ.

—1 Corinthians 15:57

I have been crucified with Christ; it is no longer I who live, but Christ lives in me; and the life which I now live in the flesh I live by faith in the Son of God, who loved me and gave Himself for me.

—Galatians 2:20

Be sober, be vigilant; because your adversary the devil walks about like a roaring lion, seeking whom he may devour. Resist him, steadfast in the faith.

—1 Peter 5:8–9

My Personal Fear Fighters

_____

_____

_____

_____

_____

_____

_____

_____

_____

_____

_____

_____

_____

_____

_____

_____

_____

_____

5

FIGHT FOR YOUR FAMILY

I**T IS OBVIOUS** that the top priority of Satan's attack in the twenty-first century is your family. If your family is the enemy's top priority, shouldn't it be yours also? In these difficult times, you must fight for the values that you cherish and the biblical and moral lifestyles you have dedicated yourself to.

A child is the only thing a man and woman can create that is eternal. When you hold that little baby that God gave you in your arms, you are holding an eternal soul. It will be alive one thousand years from now—somewhere. You must fight for the soul of that child no matter what attack of the enemy comes against it.

Does fear grip your heart when you see your children struggling with peer pressure? With temptation to give in to destructive lifestyles? Don't allow fear to overcome you. Instead, you need to fight for your family in prayer. God is with you and will work miracles for you when you pray for your family.

That is how we are fighting for our family. The world is not going to invade our home without us knowing it. We are constantly making ourselves aware of what our children are doing. Any parent who retreats in times like these, sticking their head in the proverbial sand, will witness hell invading their home. Through watching and prayer, we can keep our children safe.

When television, Internet, MySpace, and Twitter open your children to a world of evil, as parents you cannot be neutral or absent in your children's lives. You have to fight the enemy's plans for their destruction. It does no good to worry; you have to war.

As parents of five children, my wife and I are constantly checking computers, Facebook, and cell phones. My kids know that I am paying for their cell phone and that I will read their text messages. They know they cannot have any secret codes that I cannot monitor. As my wife says, "Our children do not have a private life." We are actively guarding their minds and hearts from evil to maintain our home as a safe place for them to grow up.

I love what a visiting minister told our congregation about protecting our children from harm through prayer. He said, "I'm convinced that we can't keep our children from their testimonies. When one of my children was trying some crazy stuff, God told me to tell people who asked about that child, 'He's working on his testimony.'"

When God delivers you from evil, He gives you a testimony. When your children are tempted to sin, we can call on God, engage in the fight of faith, and watch their greatest temptation turn into a glorious testimony. If you will fight, God will fight for you.

When you choose to live righteously and embrace the faith fight, God will fight for your family. He will help you to prepare a safe place where you can ride out the flood of iniquity that is rising in the land. You have to fight the good fight of faith and face down every fear and threat to your family. My parents learned the secret of preparing a safe place for their family and of fighting for the salvation of their children.

A Tribute to My Parents' "Safe Place"

I am in the ministry today because of the godly home my parents established for my siblings and me. They taught us how to pray and to read and cherish God's Word. They taught us to respect the house of God even as little children.

As a little boy, I wanted nothing more than to play with my friends at church. I remember one Sunday when I was about nine years old. My parents pastored a little church in Henderson, North Carolina. When the regular organist was not there, my mother had to play the organ. That left me free to sit in the back of the church with my friends.

One Sunday morning, Mom was playing the organ, and my

friends and I were sitting in the back. Someone had brought a little mirror, and we noticed that the sun was streaming into the church through the windows. So, we decided to have some fun with that mirror.

We would hold it just right to reflect the sunbeam onto the mirror and then into the eyes of the choir members in the front of the church. We could see them singing, and then, all of a sudden, one would go blind because of the laser beam of sunshine we shot at their eyes. We were having the biggest time you could imagine. We were laughing and completely absorbed in our little scheme.

I didn't even notice that my mother had left the organ and was marching to the back of the sanctuary where I was sitting. Suddenly, I felt someone grab my shoulder and start leading me out of the pew into the aisle. When I realized it was my mother, I felt like shouting out, "Pray, saints, pray!"

On the way out of the sanctuary, Mom pinched my shoulder and said, "I think the devil has got hold of you." I said back to her desperately, "I think he has too," meaning no disrespect. Too late, I realized that was not the right thing to say. I will spare you the rest of the story, except to say I knew I was in for good motherly discipline because of my disrespect for the house of God.

My parents maintained a safe place for me, training me and correcting me so that I learned to walk in the fear of God. They simply said "no" to the culture's advice to "just compromise and let them do what they want to do." Every time they did that, my parents were strengthening my safe place. Every time they imposed their godly standards on my choices and lifestyle, they were rescuing me from the flood of destruction that was all around me.

Even in my teenage years when I tried to rebel, Mom and Dad prayed more for me. They did the same for my two brothers and two sisters. When one of us would begin to stray from the godly principles they taught us, we knew they were fighting for us. We always had family meals together, and if Dad, who loved to eat, was not at the table, we knew he was fasting for one of us. It was a big deal. Mom and Dad usually fasted and prayed together for their children.

Usually when I tried to sin, I could not do it successfully. Others would get by with things, and I would always get caught. One day, I went with a friend and tried to get high. I smoked five joints before I could feel just a little of the "joy."

Normally, when people get high, they start talking about seeing pink elephants and gorgeous psychedelic colors. Not me. In my pitiful high state, I saw Moses, the four horses of the Apocalypse, and other dreadful sights.

When your parents are fighting for you in prayer, those prayers have such an impact that you can't even enjoy partying. It is hard to go out and enjoy sin when you are surrounded by angels assigned to you by your godly parents. They messed me up. Even while I was sleeping, they were praying for me. They fought for my soul, and today I am profoundly grateful.

According to my personality, I could have easily become an alcoholic. When I do something, I go all the way. Social drinking would have led me into alcoholism. When drugs and alcohol were confronting my young life, my parents' values and lifestyle that had formed my character to that point helped me make the right choices.

When promiscuity was presented as a legitimate option to seeking God for a life partner, the moral principles that were part of my foundation stood there protecting me. I thank God today because when the flood of evil came against my immaturity, there was a restraining force inside of me. It told me, "There will be consequences if you choose to do evil." My parents had done their task of creating a godly perspective and a righteous atmosphere that became a powerful standard for my conduct.

When they fought for God's destiny for my life, God fought for them. I am grateful to them for their perseverance in prayer as I stand to minister God's Word today. They were the force behind this ministry. They won the fight for my destiny. They were not afraid because they understood that God was fighting for them.

Years later, when I was called to ministry and began fasting and praying a lot, I asked the Lord why He was so hard on me. He answered me and said, "Because your mother is so hard on Me." I understood that if we will be hard on God through prayer and intercession for our children and grandchildren, God will be hard on them. He will intervene in their lives and keep them from evil.

As mothers and fathers, you need to fight for your children in prayer. Don't sit around in fear of what their future holds. Don't be afraid that sin might destroy their lives. Stand up in faith and fight for your family, and God will fight for you.

How to Fight for Your Family

Nehemiah, an Old Testament hero, teaches us how to fight for our families. He was leading Israel in rebuilding the walls of Jerusalem when some enemies showed up and began to threaten their lives. They tried to frighten the people, but Nehemiah challenged the families of Israel:

> Don't be afraid of them. Remember the Lord, who is great and awesome, and *fight for your brothers, your sons and your daughters, your wives and your homes.*
> —Nehemiah 4:14, niv, emphasis added

Their enemies mocked them and despised their efforts to make Jerusalem safe again. Then, they determined to attack these Jewish families, forming a secret plot to destroy them. But rather than being intimidated, the Jews protected each other as Nehemiah taught them to defend themselves.

Nehemiah instructed one-half of them to work to build the wall while the other half stood guard. Those who were working used one hand to build and the other to carry a weapon. They guarded the city day and night. This constant vigilance was necessary to keep them safe.

I can see myself as a father standing on that wall with a trowel for building in one hand and a weapon in the other. I am determined to build a successful home and family, even in a time when half of marriages end in divorce. When statistics say kids have to go through all kinds of dangerous problems, I am going to have kids who serve the Lord. I am fighting for my children, and God is fighting with me.

As you work to build walls of righteousness to protect your home, you have to arm yourselves. You have to decide you are not going to let the enemy have your family. You have to determine, "I'm going to fight for my marriage. I'm going to fight for my children. I'm going to fight the good fight—and win!"

Fighting for our five children

Now, many years after I learned my lesson from the "mirror in church" incident, my wife and I are facing similar challenges. We are determined to build a safe place for our five children. It seems that evil is more intense, the culture is more corrupt, and the influences of worldliness that bombard our children are even more powerful than when I was a child.

One summer, we planned a family trip to the beach. Our teenage girls invited some of their girlfriends to go with them. Some other families from our church happened to be at the beach that same week. Their teenage boys were friends with our girls. So, when we arrived at the beach, we sat our girls down and laid the ground rules for what was acceptable behavior at the beach with their friends.

One thing that was not to be tolerated was for our girls to go down to the beach at night with a member of the opposite sex. We wanted to be clear to everyone concerned, so we said, "Got it?" "Yes, Dad. Got it."

Then one evening, while my wife and I were absorbed in a movie, our telephone rang. One of our daughters was there with us, and she answered the phone. I paid no attention, but her mother pricked up her ears. When my wife realized that she was talking with her older sister on the phone, she became very interested. She heard our younger daughter say, "Yes, they are sitting right here."

That was suspicious! Her mother asked her who she was talking to, and she responded meekly that it was her older sister. Her mother whispered threateningly, "You tell me everything she said, or I will take your phone away for a year!" she glanced up at her mother's face and promised quickly, nodding.

After further consultation with our daughter about the phone call, my wife came to drag me away from my movie. She said we were going to take a walk down to the beach. I moaned and resisted, but she insisted. There was no saying no to that tone in her voice.

Then, instead of taking the normal walk to the beach, she led me through bushes and made me crawl on all fours, jump over a fence, and sneak all the way to the beach—in the dark! Sure enough, we found our teenage girls there with boys from other families of the church. Once again, the church kids were corrupting our perfect little angels…I rationalized.

One of the boys saw us coming and almost went into shock. He started fidgeting, and his face turned white. He couldn't think of anything to say, so he said, "Hello, Pastor. That was a great sermon last Sunday." I was not smiling. I just said, "Ah, shut up! You don't even know what I preached. Get your tail off this beach now!"

He knew he was busted, though apparently the kids had done nothing wrong, except break the rules. He put his head down and said, "Sorry, Pastor," as he walked off. My daughters knew the rules, and after speaking to them briefly, we took them back to the cabin where we emphatically made them aware of their "safe place," to the end that they would never forget!

Training, teaching, staying in their lives, and refusing to compromise—it is all part of fighting for your family and seeing God fight for you. Building a safe place against the evil influences of society that try to tempt, coerce, and deceive them is a full-time job.

STRATEGY FOR A HEALTHY HOME

No one said that building a healthy, godly family would be easy. You must be committed to winning the war that rages against your home. The battle is relentless for parents who want to establish godly foundations for your family. You can't let up your vigil. It takes time and energy to stay in your children's lives.

Do you feel overwhelmed by their peer influences? Does the fear of drugs, alcohol, and illicit sex grip your heart for your children? Fighting against destructive forces that threaten your family means you have to call on God to fight for you. Don't be intimidated by the enemy's threats; don't just sit back and let it happen. Make up your mind to work together as parents, and support each other in the fight.

My wife and I learned that we had to settle two things as a young couple. First, that we loved God. And second, that we were totally committed to each other. That means that we are committed to the church, that we fill our lives with the Word of God continually, and that we determine to raise a godly family together.

That is what young couples need to do. There might be times when you disagree and get your feelings hurt. You might say harsh things to each other, but you have to be determined to forgive and work it out. Obey the Word of God, show mercy, and strive to live in peace.

You need to tell the enemy that he has no portion and no right to your home, your children, or your marriage. I am not afraid to raise our five children in these uncertain times, because I know that as we submit our lives to God and fight for our family, God is fighting for us.

FEAR FIGHTER

Obey the Word of God, show
mercy, and strive to live in
peace.

You have to build your home with a weapon in one hand and a trowel in the other constantly. Grab a divine weapon— the name of Jesus, the Word, prayer, and praise—in one hand. Take a building instrument in the other hand, and be prepared to fight and build as the occasion arises. Begin to declare in the taunting face of the enemy, "I'm going to rebuild, and I'm going to fight until I get the victory in my own home." Speak the name of Jesus, declare the promises of God's Word, and praise Him for the victory that is coming.

If you are a single parent, you are entitled to the same protection of the promises of God for your family. It is your responsibility to fight for your family, whatever your circumstances. You need to know that you are not alone. If you submit your life to God in prayer and fasting, you will see Him preserve your children from the destructions of the enemy.

When the enemy tries to attack my family, I declare to him what Nehemiah declared to his enemies:

> The God of heaven, he will prosper us…but ye have no portion, nor right, nor memorial, in Jerusalem.
>
> —NEHEMIAH 2:20, KJV

We don't have to be afraid of what hell can do to our children. I am aware that even if I bring them up right in the fear of the Lord, hell may have a shot at them. But when it's all said and done, they know where the altar is; they know to call on the name of Jesus. And I know that He is the preserver of my home and my children; He will fight for my family.

The Word of God promises you protection against the purposes of the enemy for those who choose to obey His will. The prophet Isaiah declared, "No weapon that is formed against thee shall prosper…This is the heritage of the servants of the LORD, and their righteousness is of me, saith the LORD" (Isa. 54:17, KJV).

PERSEVERING IN THE FIGHT

Nehemiah taught the people how to fight continually for their sons and their daughters. God will prosper you and fight for you when you declare that the enemy does not have any right to your "Jerusalem"—your home and family. He cannot touch your wife. Your children do not belong to him. He has no portion in your home.

Not only did Israel win the fight for their families, but they also preserved the safety of future generations. Did you know that portions of the wall Nehemiah and Israel restored are still standing in Jerusalem today? I have been to Israel five times and have seen parts of the Jerusalem wall that date back to the rebuilding that Nehemiah directed. Their perseverance in the battle for their families gave them victory that is still evident thousands of years later.

When you build a safe place for your children, you are building multigenerational foundations upon which your grandchildren and future generations can stand. The psalmist asked the question, "If the foundations are destroyed, what can the righteous do?" (Ps. 11:3). But if you will fight, God will fight for you to keep the foundations of righteousness for your children's children and beyond.

For that to be a reality, however, you must set a guard in your home to protect it from any sneaky plan of the enemy. You cannot allow the immorality projected through any kind of media into your home. That gives the enemy access to your home. You have to protect your family from profane and unclean speech, music, or other destructive forces that try to invade your home. That requires a continual vigil and perseverance in your fight for your family's well-being.

When I do that, I may not always be the most popular person in my home. My goal is not to be popular; I am not supposed to be a buddy or best friend to my children. I am first of all their protector from evil when they cannot discern its presence because of their immaturity.

When Noah heard the word of God to build an ark to preserve his family from destruction, he obeyed God completely. He spent over a century working to build an ark of safety for his family.

Not only did he get the animals on board, but he made sure his entire family was safely on board that ark as well. The New Testament refers to Noah as the eighth person on the ark (2 Pet. 2:5, KJV). I believe that refers to the fact that Noah was the last person to board the ark.

He did not just throw down the gangplank and board that ark, hoping the other seven members of his family would go with him. Noah was the eighth person, the last one aboard. He was not just going to be rescued himself. He determined that his kids were going with him. They were the reason for his one hundred twenty years of labor on the ark. They were part of the covenant God made with him, and he was responsible for their well-being. He made sure they went with him into the safety of that ark.

I am disturbed at the way people just give up and relinquish their children to the enemy. They take a "what's the use?" attitude when their children are tempted to sin. Or they adopt an "I hope they make it" perspective. That is a cowardly way to face the onslaught of the enemy against your family. They are worth fighting for. They are eternal souls entrusted into your care.

The Bible says that Job offered ten sacrifices every day, one for each of his ten children (Job 1). I believe he called the name of each child as he made a sacrifice for them. He was putting a hedge of blood around them, fighting for his family every day.

Every day I pray for my children by name. I ask God to hedge them about with His blood. I pray for their protection and their cleansing from any evil thing they might encounter. You need to plead the blood of Jesus over your children daily. The blood of Jesus does two things: it cleanses, and it protects your home. You can build a protective hedge around your children by applying the blood of Jesus over them in prayer.

God has given you the privilege and the responsibility to raise your children. You must fight for your sons and your daughters. Fight for your husband. Fight for your wife. Fight for your daughters-in-law and your sons-in-law. Put on the whole armor of God (Eph. 6), and declare to the enemy, "You just stepped onto holy ground when you attacked my home. I'll fight you to hell and back for my babies."

How will you live your life? Will you fill it with work and activities so that someone else has to care for your family? MTV is not going to raise my babies. Babysitters are not going to raise my babies. Schools are not going to raise my babies. My wife and I are going to raise our babies in the fear of the Lord.

Give yourself and your home to God, and He will give you wisdom and power to protect your children. You don't have to live in fear for your children. God will redeem them for His purposes. You are not alone. God is with you. Even if you are a single parent, you can rest assured that God's protection is enough for your children and you.

I believe that the devil's number one priority is to destroy your home. He wants to make it miserable; he wants to tear it to pieces. The Lord made me understand that if your home is the enemy's first priority, it must be your first priority. Not your ministry. Not your career. Not recreation or the accumulation of "things." Nothing should be more important in your life than maintaining a godly home. Your number one priority is to fight for your family against the attacks of the enemy.

CLEANSING YOUR HOME

To me, one of the most amazing scriptures in the Bible about the home is found in Leviticus 14. When the children of Israel possessed their Promised Land, God told them they would live in homes they did not build. What they did not know is that those homes had been dedicated to idols.

These pagan people lived idolatrous, ungodly lives and practiced all kinds of unclean acts. They had idols hidden in the walls of their homes. They were unseen by the people but known to God. This pagan idolatry caused streaks to appear on the walls that could only be cleansed by a blood sacrifice.

> ## FEAR FIGHTER
>
> The blood of Jesus cleanses
> and protects your home.

God told Moses that when they saw greenish or reddish streaks on the walls, the house was contaminated and had to be cleansed by blood. They had to call a priest to come and make sacrifice for their home.

These streaks on the walls were called fretting leprosy. The word *fretting* relates to anger and conflict. Is there continual strife and contention in your home? Those are streaks on the wall that have to be cleansed by the blood of Christ. Otherwise, your relationships will suffer, and your home will be destroyed.

Verbal and physical abuse are streaks on the wall that must be cleansed by the blood. These hidden things in our homes attract Satan's influence against our families. You can apply the blood of Jesus to your home, and He will give grace for forgiveness and love to rule there. God wants you to experience His peace and joy in your home.

There are other ways believers allow their homes to become contaminated, causing "streaks" on the walls. Many Christian parents allow vile music with violent lyrics into their homes (knowingly or unknowingly through iPods and other devices). Some engage in addictive pornography accessed on the Internet and other kinds of media.

Some homes have allowed books on the occult, violent TV programs, and ungodly movies to have access to their homes. They cause streaks on the walls that compromise your godliness. You have to set a standard for what is acceptable to enter your home. Draw lines against your children's exposure to profanity and uncleanness.

Monitor your children's TV programs. Be vigilant about their computer use. As the priest of your home, you must continually cleanse it with the blood of Christ. If you are a single parent, you are the spiritual head of your home. Just as Job offered sacrifices for his children continually, you are responsible to cleanse your home and dedicate it to the Lord continually.

As a parent, I understand how fear can grip your heart for your children's well-being, especially during their teenage years. They are making decisions that can affect the future and their reputations for life. To combat those fears, I have determined to fight for my family. I refuse to worry about them. Through prayer, I will make it hard on God, and He will make it hard on them. I make every effort to stay in their lives, listening to their conversations and giving them direction.

ARROWS IN THE HANDS OF A WARRIOR

The psalmist declared that children are a heritage from the Lord and are like arrows in the hand of a warrior. He said that a man who has his quiver full of them is happy (Ps. 127:3–4). I began to think about arrows and what they need to be effective. This analogy makes me the bow that gives the arrow—the child—direction.

If I point my bow in the direction of alcohol, the arrow will go toward alcohol. If I point it toward getting money as its goal, it will fly toward getting rich. The arrow will go in the direction that I point it. I can't expect the arrow to go toward the church if I am not pointing it in that direction. That is simple logic.

When you teach your children to love God, the scripture says they will not be ashamed. They won't be ashamed of where they go to church or of living moral lives. When you point them toward righteous living, they will become a weapon against the devil's plans for their destruction.

Teach your children that they are not like the family down the street or the friend in school. When they say, "They all do it," tell them you are not like other families. Point their arrow toward holiness, worship, and God's calling for their life to become a pastor, evangelist, teacher, or godly employee or employer. They are destined to become godly parents who will follow your lead.

Sometimes I think we are trading the call and purpose of

God in our children's lives for the American dream. We point their arrow toward becoming a professional athlete or a powerful businessman, or toward fame in movies or the arts. If God calls them to use a career like that as a platform to bring honor to Jesus Christ, that is the right direction for that arrow. But the greatest direction for your arrow is to bring glory and honor to Christ in whatever they do.

You have to "shoot your arrows" toward truth. Teach them that there is one God. Buddha is not God. Muhammad is not God. New age philosophies do not replace God. You were created by God to walk in His truth. The apostle John said that nothing could make him happier than getting reports that his children continue diligently in the way of truth (3 John 3, THE MESSAGE)!

When you direct your children toward truth, they will understand that money is not God. Education is not God. Sports are not God. Fame is not God. Everything they value will be of God. They will know the name of God's Son, Jesus Christ, and will serve Him. They can't waiver or think there might be another way. The Bible says there is no other name given unto men whereby we can be saved (Acts 4:12).

Continually point them in the direction of truth, and they will defeat every destructive force that comes against them. You have to take charge of those precious arrows in your quiver. It is a continual fight to keep them going in the right direction, but God will fight for you when you decide to fight for your family. Pray with me that God will help you begin or intensify your battle to maintain a safe place for your family:

Dear Jesus, thank You for my family. Thank You for opening my eyes to see that You want my home to be a safe place—an ark—to give refuge against the floodwaters of sin that threaten our world today. Help me to make my family the priority that You intend it to be. I repent for being afraid to face the problems I see in my home. I determine to fight for my family, knowing that You will fight for me. Holy Spirit, please show me every unclean thing that needs to be cleansed from my life and home. I refuse to worry or be afraid. Through intercession, I will make it hard on You, God, and You will make it hard on them. Thank You. Amen.

FEAR FIGHTER'S ARSENAL

Fight for Your Family

But as for me and my house we will serve the LORD.

—JOSHUA 24:15

Behold, children are a heritage from the LORD,
The fruit of the womb is a reward.
Like arrows in the hand of a warrior,
So are the children of one's youth.

—PSALM 127:3–4

The righteous man walks in his integrity;
His children are blessed after him.

—PROVERBS 20:7

Even a child is known by his deeds,
Whether what he does is pure and right.

—PROVERBS 20:11

Train up a child in the way he should go,
And when he is old he will not depart from it.

—PROVERBS 22:6

Fathers, do not provoke your children to wrath, but bring them up in the training and admonition of the Lord.

—EPHESIANS 6:4

My Personal Fear Fighters

_____

_____

_____

_____

_____

_____

_____

_____

_____

_____

_____

_____

_____

_____

_____

_____

_____

_____

6

THE FEAR OF NOT HAVING ENOUGH

Recession. Foreclosure. Unemployment. Bankruptcy. Inflation. Fraud. Corruption. Exploding national deficit. These fear-laced words describe the economic condition of our world that is more and more dependent on a healthy global economy. Millions of people are not just hearing them; they are also living one or more of these dire financial scenarios.

It is a fact that our world continually faces difficult times of financial crisis. It is also a fact that you don't have to be afraid concerning your finances. The Word of God is still true. It says, "For God has not given you a spirit of fear, but of power and of love and of a sound mind" (2 Tim. 1:7). You don't have to be afraid of your financial situation, either present or future. Faith in God's Word during times of financial crisis will conquer all fear.

If local and national government, financial institutions, personal wealth, or productivity is your source of financial security, you may experience a terrible letdown. Your fear levels may rise to the point of causing serious physical and mental distress. It is time to evaluate your options. Do you know what the Word of God teaches about your financial provision? What promises does God give you to conquer your fear of financial ruin?

ATTACK YOUR LACK

Sometimes we are in financial difficulty because of our own poor choices or mistakes. At other times, there are situations we didn't create that make our lives difficult. There are times we can feel like victims of other peoples' decisions, of an unexpected illness or accident, or of a worldwide economic crisis that threatens our financial future. The playing field is not always level when it comes to our financial security.

Disasters strike. The good news is that God is Master in times of disaster. Whether from your poor choices or from circumstances beyond your control, when you call on God, He will resolve your financial mess. Even if your financial distress is self-inflicted, God has a plan to get you out. You don't need to be tormented by fear about your finances.

I want to show you how to attack your lack. It starts with your mentality regarding finances. Some people have a poverty mentality. They may have been raised poor or for some reason expect to be poor all their lives. They just talk about their financial lack all the time. They develop a mentality of *entitlement* that expects to receive from the wealth of others instead of from what they earn for themselves. If you have this mentality, your first attack against your financial lack is to change your thinking.

> ## FEAR FIGHTER
>
> God is Master in times of disaster.

There was a widow in the Old Testament who was destitute because of circumstances beyond her control (2 Kings 4:1). Her husband had died and left her with two sons and a pile of debt. Because of the debt, the creditor was coming to take her sons away to be his slaves. Desperate, she sent for the man of God, the prophet Elisha, and asked for his help.

Elisha asked her what she had in the house. She said she had nothing but a jar of oil. Then he told her to borrow as many empty vessels from all her neighbors as she could. She was to close the door and have her sons help her pour that little jar of oil into all those empty vessels.

When she obeyed the word of the prophet, the oil was multiplied and flowed until all the vessels were filled. Then he told her to go and sell the oil and pay her debt. There was enough left over for her family to live on the profit from that sale.

The playing field was not level for this widow. But when she called on God, He became the Master of her disaster. He has a plan for you if you will seek Him to release you from your financial disaster.

How to Qualify for God's Abundance

The Bible teaches that it is God who gives you the power to get wealth (Deut. 8:18). God told Abraham that He was going to bless him so that he could be a blessing to nations. It is God's will to give you prosperity with a purpose, to make you a blessing to others.

Are you nervous or afraid about your financial situation? You need to remind yourself that God is your source of financial provision. Start declaring, "It is God who insures my success this year. It is God who gives me the power to get wealth even in the face of my present need!"

Jesus told thirty-eight parables that deal with money management. That is five times more teaching on money than He did on prayer. There are five hundred verses about prayer and fasting, compared to two thousand on money and possessions from Jesus's teachings. Why did Jesus teach more on money than He did on prayer? Why is money so important to Jesus? Because He knows that if you do not master money, it will master you.

You do not qualify for God's abundance until you first become

His child. God loves to provide for His children more than earthly fathers do. You have to decide to become a child of God through faith in His Son, Jesus Christ. Then, all the promises of God become yours. I have five kids, and they can eat out of our refrigerator anytime. But if kids from the neighborhood came to raid our fridge, I would have a problem with that. They have their own parents who are to provide for them.

God wants to be your Father, and He wants His children to prosper—His way. The psalmist said that when you delight in God, everything you do will prosper (Ps. 1). You need to understand the generous heart of God for you to have abundance. He wants to change your poverty mentality. You have to believe His promises and confess that it is God's will for you to prosper. Your faith will set you free from fear of financial failure.

In the story of the prodigal son, the father is a picture of our heavenly Father. When that boy repented and came home, his father told his servants to kill the fat calf, bring the best robe, give him shoes, and put a ring on his son's finger. That is the heart of our heavenly Father to bless His children with His best.

One of my favorite fear fighters is the declaration of the psalmist that he was young and is now old and has not seen the righteous forsaken or his descendants begging for bread (Ps. 37:25). That divine promise is yours for your children and you to enjoy God's abundance when you live as a child of God. He has promised that no matter how old you get, He will take care of you. You will never be a beggar or a pauper. God will never forsake you when you qualify for His abundance.

When I went to India, I saw people starving in the streets. Cows mingled among the people. My mouth watered thinking of all that beefsteak running around. But they would not eat one of them because cows are considered to be gods. They worship the animal that God provided as food for their nourishment.

More than half of the grain produced in India is eaten by rats.[1] They don't kill them, because they are considered gods also. Because they do not serve the living God, they are doomed to poverty and starvation. How they need to know the wonderful news of the gospel that would set their captive hearts free!

FEAR FIGHTER

"I have been young and now am old; yet I have not seen the righteous forsaken, nor his descendants begging bread" (Ps. 37:25).

I am so glad I worship the living God who wants me to prosper. He gave all things to us to enjoy in Christ. The difference between living in prosperity and living in poverty is a choice. Choices have consequences. God told Israel that He set death and life, blessing and cursing, before them. They had to choose life or death (Deut. 30:19). It is not by chance that you are blessed; it is by choice.

Giving is a choice. Jesus said if you give, it will be given back to you according to the way that you give (Luke 6:38). Jesus taught that if you give, you will receive a "four-way gain clause": (1) good measure, (2) pressed down, (3) shaken together, and (4) running over.

Givers gain. Nothing multiplied by nothing is nothing. God multiplies seed that is sown. The Bible teaches that he who sows sparingly will also reap sparingly (2 Cor. 9:6). It is a law of harvest. Conversely, if you sow generously, you will reap generously. According to the way you sow, you will reap. This law of harvest applies to your finances as well. You will gain largely when you give largely, but you have to qualify by choosing to be a giver.

Diligence is a choice. The Bible says that we are to work six days and rest on the seventh day. There are two kinds of people God will not bless: lazy people and stingy people. You cannot be successful without hard work. God's Word does not teach an entitlement mentality that feels others owe you something. It teaches that a lazy person will live in need and have nothing, but the soul of the diligent will prosper (Prov. 13:4). The greatest way to fight poverty is to get a job.

Sin is a choice. Sin brings poverty, low living, addictions, and destroyed lives. Living under a financial curse of sin is a choice. If you choose not to give, not to work, not to be responsible for the prosperity God wants to give to His children, you will bring a curse of poverty to your life.

RESPONSIBILITY OF STEWARDSHIP

God wants you to enjoy the money He gives you. But He also wants you to understand that it comes with responsibility. When Jesus taught the parable of the talents in Matthew 25, He was teaching about how to handle money. A talent was a sum of money, and Jesus told the story of a landowner who had great possessions, which he left in charge of his servants when he went on a long journey.

The landowner, a picture of God the Father, left His servants in charge of His goods. He gave five talents to one, two talents to another, and one talent to the last, according to their ability. They were responsible for the proper investment of his funds until he returned.

The first two servants used the money wisely and increased the landowner's investment. The third buried his one talent because he was afraid. When the landowner returned, he commended the first two servants for the increase of his talents. When the third servant offered the one talent back to the landowner, he was rebuked for not at least putting it in a bank to gain interest. The landowner called him wicked and slothful for his irresponsibility. Then he took the talent and gave it to the one who had used his five talents wisely.

The money did not belong to the servants; it belonged to the landowner. They were responsible for investing it wisely. You need to have the mentality that God is the rightful owner of everything He gives you. You are the manager to use His gifts responsibly. It's God's house that you live in. The clothes you wear are God's. It's God's money you spend. You don't own it, but as a steward you have rights to use it and must take responsibility for the way you do.

As you learn to practice the principles of God's Word regarding tithing and giving, the curse of lack will be broken over your life. His promise of prosperity is based on your obedience to His Word. When you seek His will and obey His commandments, you will walk in divine destiny and enjoy the prosperity God desires for you.

RELEASE TO INCREASE

God's children historically have been prosperous. This reality is a gift of God. He wants His children to prosper. The Bible says that in Israel there was a law that every seven years Israelites who had become enslaved because of debt were to be set free (Deut. 15). This law was true only for Hebrews. If a foreigner owed you money, they would have to serve you until the debt was paid.

What was true for the children of Israel is still a valid principle for us today. God never intended for His children to be subject to slavery to debt permanently. God always deals with His children differently from people who are not walking in relationship with Him. That is one reason I am a Christian. I found out that God is for me when I live for Him.

You may be in a financial mess now, but if you are a born-again believer, God has a way out for you. Your slavery to financial loss, depression, fear, drugs, and alcohol is not a permanent state. He wants to release you to divine increase in every area of your life. Jesus came to set the captives free.

God has given promises to His children for prosperity and blessing since the earliest of times. He told Abraham that He would make him a great nation and multiply him in blessing so much that he would be a blessing to the nations. God's intention for His children is that they be blessed in every way.

If you are in a financial mess, you need to understand that your present is not your future. Your problem is temporary if you walk with God, because He intends to bless His children. God does not want you to give into a poverty mentality and think, "I will never get out of this." That is not God's voice. His voice is always a voice of freedom and hope.

The apostle Paul wrote the entire Book of Galatians to explain to us our inheritance of the promises of Abraham through Jesus Christ. As Christians, we are in the bloodline of blessing through the blood of Christ. Those blessings include financial freedom from economic slavery.

One of the great Hebrew names for God is Jehovah-Jireh, our provider. He is able to deliver you from every yoke of bondage to debt, poverty, and every kind of financial loss. If He provided release every seven years for indebted slaves in Israel, then you can believe that living under a better covenant, the blood of Jesus, He will deliver you.

Do you expect God to conform to your logic? To work according to your ability to make money or not? God is a supernatural God. He is not bound by natural circumstances. He works miracles in every realm of life for those who call on Him and believe Him. God supersedes any natural law of finance to work His miracles of prosperity in your life. He can step into your situation in an instant with supernatural provision that supersedes your logic.

The Scriptures say that when God delivered Israel from their bondage in Egypt, they plundered the Egyptians. That nation was so glad to get rid of those slaves that they freely gave them gold, silver, jewelry, livestock, and anything else they asked of them. God's people left their land of slavery rich in goods and money.

Your year of release can be just as dramatic. Don't think that what you have achieved financially is the best you can do. Dare to believe God's desire to release you to His increase. Begin to declare, "I have not done my best work. I have not achieved my greatest success yet. I have not seen my best days. God is able to take me into His promised land of blessing and purpose beyond my wildest dreams."

I don't believe everyone is destined to become a millionaire. That is the teaching of some who endorse hyperprosperity. But neither does God want you to live in financial lack, having to worry about not having enough for your next mortgage payment or to buy food for your children. If you honor God, He will honor you and provide for your needs.

PROSPERITY WITH A PURPOSE

As you learn to be a good manager of God's blessings, He has promised to increase them in your life. He doesn't just want you to gain wealth to use on your own pleasure. You cannot judge your righteousness or spirituality by how much wealth you have. Gain is not godliness. If that were true, the Mafia would be considered godly. God gives prosperity to help you fulfill His purposes in the earth.

The Scriptures teach that it is possible to live on four different levels of financial reality. God wants to move you from the lowest level to the highest as you put your faith in His promises for supernatural provision.

The bag level

Have you ever had a hole in your pocket and not known it? If you put money in it, you lose it. Haggai told the people that they were working hard but living without enough to eat or drink

(Hag. 1). They didn't have enough clothes to wear or to keep them warm. What was the problem? He said it was that they were holding on to what they made, thinking only of themselves and neglecting the house of God. They were violating God's principles of generosity and giving.

Do you have a bag level mentality? Are you earning and saving and trying to hold on to all your money? Just when you think you are getting ahead, something happens to your car. Or you get sick and have unexpected medical bills. It seems as if there is a hole in your pocket, and you never have enough.

This bag level of financial reality, where many live, is the place of lack where you never have enough. It says, "I am keeping everything I get; I am bagging it up." People with this mentality think that to get ahead they have to hold on selfishly to every penny. They are bound by the Judas spirit of greed and dishonesty.

Judas was the disciple who took care of the moneybag for Jesus's ministry. He also sold Jesus to His captors for thirty pieces of silver. He was probably one of the disciples who was upset when the woman extravagantly poured out expensive perfume on the feet of Jesus. Was he the one who called it waste that could have been used to help the poor? (See Matthew 26:9.)

Are you living on the level of financial reality where there is never enough? Holding on to everything you get will keep you in a place of lack because it violates God's principles of giving. You need to learn the secret of getting free from this financial bondage by giving, even in your time of financial lack. The good news is that you don't have to stay on the bag level. You can be released to enjoy God's increase in your personal finances.

The barrel level

In Jesus's teachings about money, He taught that those who were faithful in a little would be faithful in much (Luke 16:10). That principle is the key to learning to live in the barrel level of blessing. When all you have is a little, you have to learn to give a little. You have to overcome your fear of not having enough. Sowing seed for a harvest is the secret to reaping that harvest.

During the famine in Israel that was announced by Elijah, God told Elijah to leave the brook where He had fed him supernaturally by ravens. He told him to go and find a widow in Zarephath who would provide for him (1 Kings 17).

When Elijah found the widow, he asked her to bring him some water and a morsel of bread. She told him that she did not have any bread. She had a handful of flour in the barrel and a little oil in a jar. She was gathering sticks to cook it for her and her son to eat it and die.

Elijah said to her, "**Do not fear**; go and do as you have said, but make me a small cake from it first, and bring it to me" (1 Kings 17:13, emphasis added). Then he told her that if she did that, the promise of God to her was that the barrel of flour would not be used up or the jar of oil run dry until the famine was over.

So the widow made a cake for Elijah first. She used everything she had to give to God's servant as he had asked. She and her son survived the famine for many days with the flour and oil that was supernaturally refilled in the barrel and jar.

If you want to get out of the bag level into the barrel level, you are going to have to let fear go and act in faith. You have to give in the face of your own need. It is not logical. Why would I give when I don't have enough for myself? Because that puts you into miracle territory. Miracles happen in miracle territory! That is the place where you give in faith in obedience to God.

Elijah told the widow to make him a cake first. He was saying to her, "Move into miracle territory!" The moment she obeyed, she moved from bag level of not having enough to barrel level of having just enough. She sowed one cake in obedience, and God gave her a miraculous harvest that met her needs every day until the famine ended.

I like to imagine her friends coming to her home to see this widow open her barrel and take out another day's supply of meal. They watched her go to her empty jar of oil and pour out enough for that day's baking. They saw a supernatural miracle of God's provision. She told them the story again about making her last cake for the prophet who asked her to give to him first. They gave thanks to God for teaching her how to move into miracle territory through giving.

If you are living in the bag level, God wants you to move into the barrel level, where you have enough to pay bills and provide for your family. That widow was eating her last meal. She did not have enough to survive another day...until she gave to the prophet in obedience. Then God prospered her on a new level of miraculous provision. It was just enough, but that was so much better than not having enough.

The barrel level is a blessing of God to keep you from financial lack. You need to be thankful that God has given you just enough...that you don't have to live without enough for your bills...that you have a home and car and the necessities of life. Thank God that you are not living on the bag level. You have moved into miracle territory by learning to give in obedience to God's principles.

I don't believe God wants you to just have enough to pay your bills and meet your family's needs. It is still selfish to think only of yourselves and your needs. You cannot help those less fortunate when you live with just enough for yourselves in your barrel. God wants you to know His great giving heart of generosity—being able to give to the needs of others.

If you have been stuck at the barrel level, where at the end of the month you make all your payments but have nothing left over, you need to ask God to move you to the third level of financial reality—the basket level.

The basket level

Do you remember the little boy who offered his lunch to Jesus to feed the multitude? He got up that morning and put five little loaves of bread and two fish in his lunch basket. Then he followed the crowd to hear a Galilean by the name of Jesus preach (Mark 6).

The Bible says that after Jesus had taught the multitude of more than five thousand people, they were hungry. Jesus asked His disciples to feed them. They were astonished at the suggestion to feed all those people. Their answer was to send them away. They told Jesus that all the food they had seen was a little boy's lunch of five loaves of bread and two fish. Jesus told them to bring it to Him.

The Bible says that Jesus took the loaves and fish, blessed them, broke them, and then gave them to the people. This is the same process that you must go through if you want to fulfill the purposes of God for your life.

First, He takes you out of sin, sets you free, and blesses you. This is the part of the process we love. It feels so good to be free from sin and to have the blessing of God on our lives. Then, He begins the breaking process to change our thinking, our selfish desires, and our wrong choices. That is the part we want to skip. But He is breaking you because He wants to "give" you to the people.

God wants to make you a blessing to others, to your community, and even to the nations of the world. When that little boy offered his lunch to the Master, Jesus blessed his basket and used it to satisfy his whole community. All the people were fed from the miraculous multiplication of that little lunch, and there were twelve basketfuls left over!

I think there were twelve basketfuls so that each of the disciples could carry one. I like to imagine that little boy going home to his mother with the disciples following him. His mother sees them and asks what has happened. He says he went to hear Jesus and gave Him his lunch to feed five thousand people. These twelve basketfuls were left over from when Jesus blessed his lunch. They had food for many days to come.

When you give what you have to God, who is the rightful owner, He will bless it and multiply it to meet every need. God wants to move you personally and the entire body of Christ from the barrel level of having just enough to the basket level of providing for the needs of others.

After that community was blessed, the little boy showed up at home with basketfuls left over! If you are living in the barrel level of having just enough, you need to know there is another level that is more than enough! God wants to release you to increase.

One of my family's most memorable Christmases was when we were able to give extravagantly to a deserving family. Our church had several Christmas trees on the stage as decoration during the Christmas season. One of our pastors told me that a single mother of three children had asked if she could just borrow one of those trees for her children's Christmas.

I investigated her situation and realized that she was genuinely trying to give her children all she could on her limited income. She had recently suffered a divorce because of domestic violence and an abusive relationship.

So, on Christmas Eve, my wife and children went with me to Toys "R" Us and began to do Christmas shopping for this family. My children picked out gifts for the children, and we bought decorations and a Christmas tree for them. We arrived at their home with trucks full of gifts for this family. When we delivered all the packages and decorations, we turned to leave. Once outside the apartment, we heard this mother begin to shout her thanksgiving to God. We listened to the squeals of the children, and our hearts were warmed with gratitude to God that we were blessed to bless others.

We need to become people who are looking to bless others. Then God will increase our basket level until it reaches beyond it to the fourth level of financial reality—the barn level.

The barn level

If God can trust you with more than enough so that you are able to give to others, He will move you to an even greater level of prosperity. God wants you to think BIG! You are completely victorious over your fear of financial failure when you understand that your prosperity is for a purpose. Wealth is not about becoming "fat cats." It is about becoming a blessing to others.

When Joseph was delivered from prison and appointed by Pharaoh as the second in command in Egypt, God used him to create food storage centers that would preserve nations during a time of famine. The barns of food that Joseph stored during the seven good years of harvest helped feed the whole world during the seven bad years of famine.

God wants to raise some of you to the barn level. He knows that if He gets it *to* you, He can get it to flow *through* you to touch people all over the world with the truth of the gospel as well as with material blessing.

There are people in my church that I have pastored for twenty years who were living between the bag and barrel levels years ago. They were hard working and learning to give out of their need. Now, they have become multimillionaires who continue to give more and more to reaching lost souls with the gospel.

God did not move them from bag level to barn level overnight. They went through His process of giving themselves to Him and allowing Him to break them to use them for His purposes. Out of that brokenness, He is pouring His blessing through lives. The secret of moving from the bag level of not having enough to the barn level of having enough for the nations, in a word, is *obedience.*

No matter what level of financial reality you are living in, God already has more than enough for your needs. You don't have to fear your financial situation. God knows how to move you from financial lack to abundance. The only thing that can limit you is in your own faith level. When God says move, you have to act in faith to move into His miracle territory.

You may say, "Well, I am retired and live on a fixed income." Not in God. That is not a limitation to God when you move in faith to what He asks you to do. "Well, the economy is down." Do you remember the woman living in famine? Her famine was over when she obeyed what the prophet told her to do, to give first out of her need.

You may be about to give birth to a miracle. It is time to get out of the level of lack or of just getting by and allow God to release into your life His resources. If you will obey God and quit holding on to what you have, He will release His provision into your hands so that you can bless others.

I understand that some have taken a "prosperity message" to the extreme. I do not believe in that, but I do believe in prosperity with a purpose. I believe what the Bible teaches about the law of sowing and reaping, and I believe Jesus's teaching about giving. He did not only teach giving; He gave His life to break the curse of sin over your life. He died to give you a quality of abundant life, not just for eternity—but also for now. He wants to bless you and make you a blessing to others.

The Bible warns against greed and the love of money, calling the love of money the root of all evil (1 Tim. 6:10). You need to guard against loving money more than you love God. God wants to bless your life, not just with money, but also with great love for Him and for His Word. He wants to give you His love for the lost souls in the world. When you seek God first and walk in

His commandments, He will release supernatural resources into your life.

> ## FEAR FIGHTER
>
> God knows how to move you from financial lack to abundance.

One of my favorite psalms is Psalm 112, which lists all the blessings God wants to give to us. The prerequisite of receiving His blessings is to walk in the fear of the Lord and delight in His commandments. I fear God. I reverence God and honor Him. I take His Word seriously. According to His Word, God delights in the person who does that.

He delights in you when you read His Word and love it with all your heart. Speak His Word, and walk in His commandments. Begin to say, "I know that God wants to bless me." His promises to you are powerful when you love Him. Your children will be mighty and blessed. You will not be afraid of evil tidings because you are trusting in the Lord. You will guide your affairs with discretion, and you will triumph over your enemies. (See Psalm 112, THE MESSAGE.)

Fear of not having enough is a terrible enemy. God does not want you to live your life on the bag level. His will is to bless you to be a blessing to others. I will not pastor a bag-level church. God has raised up the body of Christ to reach the nations with the good news of the gospel. That will take barn-level resources.

A testimony of grace

When I first began to pastor our church, I decided we would not have a bag mentality, meaning we would not ignore the needs of the poor and destitute in our community and in the world. We began to feed the poor and minister to the needy. We determined to become a church characterized by generosity that would give millions of dollars to world missions.

There were times when we were in major building programs and needed money for our concerns. The bag mentality says to satisfy first the needs of your own and to clutch the moneybag to yourself without helping others. But during those times, we continued to give, and we increased more and more. As we continued to give, we progressed from a mentality of not having enough to having more than enough. Today, our ministry is totally debt free, and we are able to give like never before.

By God's grace we have left the bag level behind and are living in the barn level that is able to supply for the needs of others. Our church is taking resources to Haiti to feed impoverished children there. We are working with a malnutrition center to give 3.2 million meals to the neediest children every year. God spoke to us to tithe on the income from our television ministry and give to the nations. We will be doing the same in Africa as well.

In our area, we support Freedom From Addiction ministries for men, women, and teens. Other outreach ministries are being funded out of our barn-level resources as a church. Why does God give us the ability to get wealth? So that He can establish His covenant on the earth. He wants us to take the gospel to every creature.

If you want to have a new beginning in the area of finances and successfully combat your fear of financial lack, please pray this prayer with all your heart:

Dear Jesus, thank You for Your wonderful promises to care for Your children as a heavenly Father. I come to embrace Your Word and to seek first Your kingdom. I renounce a spirit of poverty and ask You to release Your levels of prosperity in my life as I obey Your Word. Help me to give with a generous heart. Don't let me stop at having just enough, but allow me the privilege of giving to others as well. I believe You will show me the strategies I need for my employment and my business to combat any financial lack that I will face now or in the future. Keep me from covetousness and greed, and make me a blessing to my community and beyond. Amen.

The Fear of Not Having Enough

Oh, fear the LORD, you His saints!
There is no want to those who fear Him.
The young lions lack and suffer hunger;
But those who seek the LORD shall not lack any good
  thing.

—PSALM 34:9–10

Let the LORD be magnified,
Who has pleasure in the prosperity of his servant.

—PSALM 35:27

Praise the LORD!

Blessed is the man who fears the LORD,
Who delights greatly in His commandments.

His descendants will be mighty on earth;
The generation of the upright will be blessed.
Wealth and riches will be in his house,
And his righteousness endures forever....

He will not be afraid of evil tidings;
His heart is steadfast, trusting in the LORD.

—PSALM 112:1–3, 7

Now if God so clothes the grass of the field, which today is, and tomorrow is thrown into the oven, will He not much more clothe you?

—MATTHEW 6:30

Beloved, I pray that you may prosper in all things and be in health, just as your soul prospers.

—3 JOHN 2

My Personal Fear Fighters

_____

_____

_____

_____

_____

_____

_____

_____

_____

_____

_____

_____

_____

_____

_____

_____

_____

7

FIGHTING THE FEAR OF FAILURE

AILURE. THERE IS hardly a more terrifying word in the human language. Failing economy, failing marriage, failing grades, failing to fulfill your dreams. The fear of failure is so paralyzing that it keeps many people from even reaching for their dreams; they simply cannot face the risk of trying and failing.

What is your dream? Are you afraid to risk failure to walk in destiny? You have to become a fear fighter if you expect to walk in the success God has for you. Only then can you live in His purpose and destiny where you will know ultimate fulfillment in life.

Fear of failure is listed among the top ten worst human fears. It ranks alongside other "learned" fears that include the fear of public speaking, rejection, disapproval, making mistakes, aloneness, financial problems, and death.[1]

Did you know that there are over two thousand fears or phobias that have been identified in human experience? Yet, according to psychologists, human beings are born with just two basic fears: the fear of loud noises and the fear of falling. All other fears have to be learned.[2]

That means you were not born with a fear of failure. You learned to be afraid of failing because of what you have experienced in life. Failure was not God's intention for mankind. Fear entered the human race because of sin.

The first thing Adam did after he sinned was run and hide from the presence of God. When God came to commune with him in the cool of the day, Adam was nowhere to be found. God called to him, and Adam answered, "I heard Your voice in the garden, and **I was afraid** because I was naked; and I hid myself" (Gen. 3:10, emphasis added).

The primary evil that Satan released into the earth through sin was fear. Now, people suffer the torment of all kinds of fears that paralyze them, robbing them of a victorious life. Fear will keep you from trying because you might fail. You might look foolish, or you might be rejected.

Do you remember the Michael Jackson album *Thriller*? This

hit song and music video is listed in the *Guinness Book of Records* (2006) as the most successful music video. It focuses on the fear of the thriller movies. Why was it so popular? Because it was centered on fear, and everybody can relate to fear.

But God does not want you to be paralyzed by fear. Did you know that the Bible says, "Fear not," or "Be not afraid," 365 times? That is one "fear not" for every day of the year. When you get up every morning, there is a "fear not" from God waiting for you no matter what your day brings!

I have had to use those "fear not" promises to give me courage to become what God wants me to be. When I was young, I was shy and backward. I would not be in the ministry today if God had not helped me overcome my fear of failure.

SCARY MOMENTS CAN BE GREAT OPPORTUNITIES

Some of my scariest moments have given me my greatest opportunities. When the Lord called me to preach, I was traveling with my brother, who was preaching as an evangelist. He invited me to preach one night of the revival services where he was ministering. For an entire week before that opportunity, I was so nervous and frightened that I became sick.

You will not meet a more shy, backward, introverted person than I was at that time. My heart pounded just to think of getting up in front of people. I fasted and prayed that week, and I still remember the terror I felt that day when we got into the car and my brother drove me to that service where I was to preach my first sermon.

I was agonizing in the passenger seat, thinking something like, "This is not happening. It is simply not happening." Here I am about to get up in front of forty people and preach. It might as well have been forty thousand people, as frightened as I was. My mind was racing. I thought to myself, "What do you think you are doing? You won't remember a word you are supposed to preach." I was sure that I was going to look foolish. What if I failed?

The pastor of the church introduced me and announced that I was coming to preach my first sermon. I was cringing in my seat, afraid that I was going to embarrass myself and look stupid. But I defied my fear. I preached that sermon. It was a pitiful sermon, but years later, I realized that by overcoming one of my scariest moments, I had stepped into my greatest opportunity. Destiny was opened to me through that opportunity.

Another one of my scariest moments was when I met my wife. I got up the courage to ask her for a date, and she accepted. I was relieved and grateful. After we had dated a few times, I realized that we were becoming seriously interested in one another. I was a traveling evangelist at the time and was ministering at a revival in Alabama. So, I asked her to try to arrange to travel to the services for the weekend to see me. Her aunt and uncle offered to bring her, and the arrangements were finalized.

Before they left to come to Alabama, her mother told her that she knew I was going to tell her that I loved her during the visit with me. Of course, I did not know anything about that until later.

I had asked her to go out for dinner with me after the service along with her aunt and uncle. Then, later that evening, we were sitting alone talking. As the conversation progressed, I took the opportunity to say to her, "I love you."

The conversation ended abruptly. She went completely silent for what seemed an eternity. Immediately, I was gripped with fear. I didn't know she was in shock, thinking about what her mother had told her. I just knew that I had told her I loved her and thought that her silence meant she did not feel the same way.

So, I started to panic, thinking I must have misread her feelings and that she was going to reject my love. Quickly, I tried to find a way to take back my words. I fumbled around trying to say something to put her at ease. I managed, "You know, when someone says they love you, it can mean many things, like, 'I've never felt this way before' or 'I care deeply for you.' It doesn't necessarily mean that I am in love with you." I was fighting desperately for a way out of my dilemma when she interrupted me.

Through my fog of fear I heard her say, "I love you too." Relief flooded my mind and heart, and I blurted out, "OK, I really do love you." As they say, the rest is history. We have laughed many times about that moment. But what if I had given in to the fear of rejection? What if I had not risked telling her how I felt? I could have missed out on the great love of my life.

Then, when I asked her to marry me, I was scared to death. I thought, "What if she has had second thoughts? What if she says no?" But she said yes, and that scary moment led to one of the best opportunities of my life—the honeymoon. We have been married for twenty-two years and have five great kids. What if

I had missed all of that by giving into fear? **Fear fighters take advantage of opportunities.**

If you are single, don't be afraid to strike up a conversation. Be free to offer friendship to see if God will let you develop a meaningful relationship. For me, as shy and backward as I was, just to approach her was a big deal. But I stepped out of my fear and took the risk, and I am so glad I did. You don't know what you may be missing if you are allowing fear of rejection to paralyze you.

Later, we left the denomination where we started in ministry because God spoke to us to go to a small church in Gainesville. My mind was screaming at me to go back home and be safe in the ministry where we were comfortable. But God gave us courage to leave everything familiar that we loved to begin to minister at Free Chapel in Gainesville. God has been with us to give us good success.

Every expansion of this ministry has required that I overcome the fear that would keep us playing it safe. Sometimes it seemed impossible to do what God had told us to do. Building facilities that cost millions of dollars to accommodate the vision God has given us requires courage. Establishing community outreaches and going to the nations has been a challenge every step of the way. Fear would have kept us from fruitfulness in these areas.

Then, recently God opened an opportunity to pastor in Orange County. When I first got on the plane to fly to California, my mind was telling me that I did not know what I was doing. How could I pastor a church on the East Coast and another on the West Coast both on the same day?

Yet, now the Orange County church has grown to several thousand people and involves effective outreaches to the community.

If God says to do something, then you need to do it and shame the devil. Fight the fear that he tries to put in your way. *Fear fighters take advantage of opportunities.*

When I look back at that first sermon I preached in that little country church, I realize that message was huge. It was a gift of God to give me an opportunity to enter into destiny. Now, God has given me the opportunity to preach to multitudes of people through travel and television. It all goes back to that first message I preached in one of my scariest moments.

When I remember asking my wife for our first date, I am aware that overcoming that scary moment opened a wonderful door for my future. Daring to fight my fear has resulted in life opportunities to walk in destiny that would have been lost otherwise.

What about you? I wonder what opportunities you are backing down from that God has placed in your life to promote you to unbelievable success. What have you been afraid to do that might be a God-given opportunity for your future? God wants you to take advantage of your opportunities. He wants you to experience success of unbelievable proportions if you will fight your fear and take a risk.

The odds may be against you. Family may oppose you. You may think you are being foolish, and the outcome may be questionable. But if you are waiting for a perfect time with little or no risk of failure, you will not move into your God-given destiny. It always comes with risk.

What may seem to be an insignificant opportunity, like my first sermon, could be a big doorway swinging on one little hinge— your decision to take advantage of that small opportunity.

WHAT IS YOUR CONTRIBUTION?

Thomas Edison failed at six thousand attempts to make an electric light bulb that would work. On one occasion, a young journalist asked Edison why he kept trying and failing to make light by using electricity: "Don't you know that gas lights are with us to stay?" Edison replied, "I have not failed. I've just found ten thousand ways that won't work."[3]

Raymond Kroc had little success in a number of business ventures before he became acquainted with the McDonald brothers' local hamburger restaurants. He was traveling across the country, selling multimixer milkshake machines. After working with them for a while, Kroc risked everything to purchase the McDonald brothers' hamburger restaurants. He implemented Henry Ford's assembly line idea into his restaurants, changing the way hamburgers were made. Through his efforts, the McDonald's golden arches were born.[4]

> ## FEAR FIGHTER
>
> Fear of failure makes you hide
> from opportunity.

What would have happened to our twenty-first-century scientific progress if Thomas Edison had quit his experiments with the light bulb after ten thousand failures? How many McDonald's hamburgers and fries would you have eaten if Ray Kroc had not overcome his failure in business? They refused to accept failure and kept seeking greater opportunity for their potential success.

Will you make your contribution to the world as God intended? I believe one of the wealthiest places in the world is the graveyard. How many people have taken their potential for writing a book, composing music, curing disease, or inventing a vital instrument to the grave with them because of fear? How many people never achieve anything because they are afraid they will look foolish trying? Fear of failure makes you hide from opportunity.

How Do You Define Failure?

To *fail*, according to Webster, means "to fall short, to be unsuccessful, to disappoint expectations, to be inadequate or become bankrupt." According to that definition, the failure rate of the human race is 100 percent!

It is impossible as a human being to eliminate failure from your life. So the real question is: What will you do when you fail? In a relationship? In business? In reaching your personal goals? Will you give in to fear of failure and quit trying?

You have to become a fear fighter. Unless you decide to fight your fear of failure, you will become paralyzed at the prospect of taking a risk. The important thing to remember when you fail is not to quit. History shows that failure can actually become a catalyst to propel you to success.

Napoleon was forty-second in his class of forty-three, but he led his army successfully to conquer the world. George Washington lost two-thirds of his military battles but won the Revolutionary War against overwhelming odds. Abraham

Lincoln's list of failures in life exceeded his successes before he became one of the greatest presidents of the United States in 1861. Here are some of the failures he experienced:

Abraham Lincoln's Failures

1832—Lost job, defeated for state legislature
1833—Failed in business
1835—Sweetheart died
1836—Had nervous breakdown
1838—Defeated for Illinois House Speaker
1843—Defeated for nomination for Congress
1848—Lost renomination
1854—Defeated for U.S. Senate
1856—Defeated for nomination for vice president
1858—Again defeated for U.S. Senate[5]

Albert Einstein was considered a dunce and told to switch from his studies in physics to some other subject. Today his name is synonymous with the term *genius*. He is credited with discovering the theory of relativity and is called the *Father of the Atomic Age*. The scientific community calls him the greatest scientist since Sir Isaac Newton.[6]

When you think of George Washington, Abraham Lincoln, or Albert Einstein, you probably do not remember their failures. You remember their contributions to the world. Yet, how would history be changed if their successes had been aborted because they quit when they first failed?

You need to realize that failure is not final. The Bible says that a righteous man may fall seven times and will rise again (Prov.

24:16). And failure is not fatal. You can begin again after failure. It is the fear of failure that could prove fatal to your goals in life. Fear will keep you from trying again. You need to realize that failure is not final.

In baseball, the superstars fail to hit the ball 70 percent of the time. If they maintain a batting average of three hundred or better, they are considered the best in the game. That means that for every one thousand times they come to bat, they will fail to get on base seven hundred times. These athletic champions have to live with that enormous rate of failure every day.

Roger Bannister, a young medical student at Oxford, wanted to be a part of the track team. He worked hard to become fit. And in 1952, he ran in the Olympics and failed to win. He did not finish higher than fourth place and failed to earn a medal. But, Roger Bannister did not quit in the face of his failure.

Experts had concluded that it was not humanly possible to run the mile in under four minutes. Yet, that was Bannister's goal. And on May 6, 1954, he became the first man to run a mile under four minutes. His time was 3 minutes 59.4 seconds. He refused to accept the experts' impossibility thinking. After Bannister's success, other athletes were inspired to break the four-minute mile barrier as well.[7]

BENEFITS OF FAILURE

If you don't quit when you fail, you will ultimately succeed in life. When babies start learning to walk, they begin by hitting every piece of furniture in the house. Falling and getting up, then falling again and getting up again—until they have mastered the balance they need to walk.

Life is like that. You have to decide to keep getting up every time you fall. Keep looking forward. Don't waste your time lamenting past failure. You have goals to reach that need all of your energy.

Failure actually has some great benefits to work in your life. Someone has wisely concluded: "It is a mistake to suppose that people succeed through success; they often succeed through failures."[8]

The psalmist said it was good for him to fail because through his failure he learned the consequences of his actions. He recognized that he was going in the wrong direction and could change it to become pleasing to God and successful in life (Ps. 119:6–7).

When people fail in one area, it drives them to explore other avenues of success. Most of life's successes are based on the principle of trial and error. Remember, failure is not falling short of your goal. Failure is simply not making the effort.

Sometimes failing will actually help you discover your area of success. For example, when you hate your job, you will likely fail in it. Yet, in losing that hated position, you may be pressed to pursue what you really like to do.

Nathaniel Hawthorne studied to become a successful writer. However, his first novel was unsuccessful. He could not earn a living at writing, and he wanted to get married. So, Hawthorne took a job as a surveyor to pay the bills. But he was eventually dismissed from that position.

Desperate, he turned back to writing, which he loved, knowing he must make a living from it. He wrote diligently and authored his famous novel *The Scarlet Letter*. It was an immediate success.

From that time on, Hawthorne was able to enjoy his coveted career as a writer.[9]

Another benefit to failure is that it will make you less judgmental. When you fail, you become more sympathetic with other people's failures. You don't kick people when they are down anymore, saying things like, "I don't believe they did that." You know how it hurts to fail, and you feel their pain because of what you have experienced.

Don't allow fear of failure to rob you of productivity and the joys of life. Be willing to fail and learn from your experience. You can't live a perfect life without making any messes.

The Bible uses agricultural language to say that to be productive you have to put up with a messy stall. If the stall is empty, it remains clean. But where oxen are, there will be some mess (Prov. 14:4). Do you want to be productive or have a clean stall?

If you decide to get married and have children, I can guarantee you that you will experience some *messes*. It is inevitable that children will *mess up the stall*. That comes with the blessing of family. Children come complete with a problem quotient. Your option is to live by yourself and enjoy a less complicated life, or to accept the problems that come with having a family—along with the joys.

The answer to overcoming all fear is to be willing to take risks. That can be scary sometimes. A fear fighter will sometimes feel afraid. The psalmist declared: "Whenever I am afraid, I will trust in You" (Ps. 56:3). That is how you overcome fear of failure and live a happy, productive life.

FIGHT FEAR WITH COURAGE AS JOSHUA DID

When my dad died suddenly at age fifty-six, he left behind a congregation that had looked to him as their *Moses*. I knew that fear had paralyzed them and kept them from their destiny as a church. After his funeral, God gave me a message for that church that would help them move ahead into their promised land.

I preached about Joshua's encounter with God after Moses's death. God told Joshua four times not to be afraid. And He gave him four reasons for not giving into fear. God knew the biggest enemy he would face would not be the giants in the land—it would be the little voices inside telling him he could not do it. It would be the voices of fear screaming, "Who do you think you are? You are not able."

Are you facing a hard situation? Have your circumstances changed unexpectedly? You have to be willing to face down those frightening voices and take a risk to move forward into your destiny. You cannot give into the spirit of timidity and draw back when times get tough.

God was giving Joshua a pep talk about overcoming fear. He could have told Joshua how to assemble a great army and how to be a great leader. But the one thing He told him was not to allow a spirit of fear to get inside of him. If a spirit of fear begins to dominate you, it will make you draw back from the victory God has for you.

God has all power to work through you when you refuse fear. You have to become a fear fighter to face the *giants*. Then God will fight for you and win the battle. God is saying to you what He said to Joshua. If you will be bold to obey whatever He tells you to do, you will continue to win! If you can stay free from the spirit of fear, nothing can defeat you.

Reason 1: Courage for the people's sake

First, God told Joshua to be strong and very courageous *for the people's sake* (Josh. 1:6). When you face life with courage and follow God with all your heart, there are others around you who will benefit from your success. Your family, friends, and others whom you influence will be able to follow you into the promised land because of your witness, your godly decisions, and your courage to take risks and become a fear fighter.

> ## FEAR FIGHTER
> God can fix anything as long as you confront the situation in His powerful name.

Your life is not just about you getting into your promised land and fulfilling your destiny. No one lives life in isolation. Your marriage, your children, your employer or employees, friends, and even lost souls around you are all watching you. They want to see if you will face trouble with courage or will buckle before it in fear. They can learn from you how to overcome fear as they see you courageously face obstacles to your success.

God spoke this reality to my heart in one of the darkest valleys I ever walked as a pastor. There was a battle raging against my ministry and the church. Mental, emotional, and physical fatigue overwhelmed me. There seemed to be little possible victory or reward in the face of overwhelming odds.

The Lord said to me: "Fear not, *for the people's sake.*" His Word helped me to summon supernatural courage not to give up for their sake. And today God has won that overwhelming battle and given us a harvest of souls many times greater than I could have imagined. Every time faith is tested and courage prevails, it grows stronger and is equipped for greater victories to come.

Because the children of Israel crossed over into their Promised Land centuries ago, we are able to enter our promised land in Christ. They are part of our history as God's plan to bring forth the Messiah through that nation. We needed for them to succeed in order to fulfill God's plan for a Savior.

In that same way, there are people attached to your life, and God needs you to succeed because they are depending on you. You are not just fighting fear because of what you get out of it. God has attached others to your dream and destiny. Don't underestimate the power your life will have on future generations when you overcome fear...*for the people's sake.*

Reason 2: Courage for your sake

God told Joshua to be fearless *for his own sake.* He told Joshua not to be afraid so that he could prosper everywhere he went (v. 7). He had been prepared in the wilderness and mentored by Moses to take Israel into the Promised Land. God did not want the fear of failure to paralyze Joshua from being able to accomplish the tremendous task that lay before him.

Are you cringing before an opportunity that seems too big for you? If you have committed your life to Christ, you can expect

Him to give you the ability and resources you need to succeed. Your main goal is to resist fear and trust God to take you through that door of opportunity.

God had a lot invested in Joshua. The success or failure of an entire nation rested on his shoulders. He reminded Joshua to be fearless not only for the people's sake but also for his own sake, so that he would be prosperous wherever he went.

God has invested a lot in you too. As His child, you need to trust Him to give you good success for your sake. It is God's desire to prosper you in all you do.

Reason 3: Courage for the Lord's sake

God told Joshua not to be afraid *for the Lord's sake* (v. 9). He promised Joshua that He was with him wherever he went. The Lord had a bigger stake in Israel's success than they did. His eternal plan to bring forth the Messiah depended on the success of Israel. God was going to do His part to make these slaves into a nation that served the true God.

Pagan nations all around had observed the supernatural plagues God brought to deliver His people from Egypt. If they failed now to conquer their Promised Land, their failure would bring reproach to His great name. God needed Joshua to exhibit great courage *for the Lord's sake.*

God's reputation is on the line when He makes you a promise. If you fail to inherit His promises through fear, your failure ultimately affects the great heart of God. He loves you and has ordained for you to walk in His ways and fulfill your destiny by trusting in His great love. And He has a plan for your success.

Reason 4: Courage for the enemies' sake

God told Joshua not to be afraid *for the enemies' sake* (v. 18). God knew there were enemies waiting for this people. He told Joshua to display strength and courage when facing them. He promised to be with him and fight for him. Joshua just needed to conquer fear for the enemies' sake.

For your enemies' sake, God wants to prove His victory in your life. King David wrote: "You prepare a table before me in the presence of my enemies; You anoint my head with oil; my cup runs over" (Ps. 23:5). God vindicates His servants when they refuse to fear their enemies.

Sometimes it is good to have enemies. An enemy can press you into victory where a friend cannot. Who would ever have heard of David without Goliath? Would you have known about Moses if there had been no Pharaoh oppressing God's people? And what would you know about Esther without Haman's evil plot against the Jews?

What is your dream? Is there an enemy standing between you and its fulfillment? Dare to confront your enemy without fear or intimidation, and it will become an instrument in God's hand to press you into your destiny.

Your heavenly Father is more zealous to protect you from your enemies than you are to protect your children from the school bully. When you submit to His lordship, He takes responsibility to fight for you. Sometimes God will bless you just because the enemy has come against you. It's like He says, "I'm not going to let you fail because you have so many enemies." You don't ever have to be afraid.

When Absalom, David's son, committed treason and drove his father from his throne, a man named Shimei followed along. He cursed David continually and threw stones at him. David's servant asked permission to kill Shimei. But David said, "Let him alone, and let him curse...It may be that the LORD will look on my affliction, and that the LORD will repay me with good for his cursing this day" (2 Sam. 16:11–12). Absalom died that day, and the throne was restored to David. Once again God did prepare a table for David in the presence of his enemies.

My dad's congregation was encouraged by this message to become fear fighters. That church became a larger, more powerful church than ever before. They did not draw back in fear. They went forward in the courage that God gave them to walk in their destiny.

WILL YOU FIGHT FOR YOUR "BEAN PATCH"?

King David showed his wisdom by surrounding himself with men of character and integrity. They were fearless men who were willing to die for their convictions. One of those men was named Shammah. He took a stand by himself in a field of lentils and fought the Philistines when everyone else ran away. He was devoted to David and fought alone against great odds to defend a patch of beans.

Why would a man be willing to die for a bean patch? Surely it was not because of the monetary value of those lentils. That ordinary bean patch was not precious; it was pivotal. Shammah understood that if he compromised that position, the enemy would keep coming and take more territory for themselves.

If he gave up the field, what would be next? His home? His children? His city? There is a powerful lesson in standing alone against fear. The moment you compromise one inch to fear, you will have to compromise more territory. And before you know it, you will lose everything you ever had in God because you did not take a stand.

What convictions have you compromised? Maybe it seems like a small thing—a glance at a pornographic magazine, using an expletive at work, cheating on your taxes. Understand that those seemingly small compromises are pivotal to your Christian life. When you give up little convictions in your life…little acts of obedience that no one notices, it becomes easier to compromise with bigger issues of life.

You have to decide to stand firm in your *bean patch* to defeat the enemy and keep him from taking more valuable *territory* in your life. As Shammah defended that field, killing the Philistine enemies, God brought about a great victory. That death-defying battle became an opportunity for Shammah. He did not merely defeat the enemy that day; he also walked into his destiny to become one of David's mighty men.

You need to be like Shammah. Station yourself to fight the enemy alone when others flee. Stand firm for your smallest convictions even when others compromise with the enemy. That's how you aid the forces of righteousness in the unseen battle that God fights for you.

The only thing that keeps evil forces from fulfilling their assignments in you and your family is to put your foot down and say, "I may look like a fool, but this bean patch matters!" Your convictions matter!

Don't let any place of fear lodge in your heart without taking a stand against it. Do it just because it is right. Live in the principles of freedom and truth, and you will make a greater impact on others' lives than you ever dreamed possible. Nothing is too small to defend against the enemy's attack.

THE BUTTERFLY EFFECT

Have you heard of the scientific term called the *butterfly effect*? It is a term in physics that describes how tiny changes in initial conditions (such as the flap of a butterfly's wings) can have large-scale effects on the development of weather thousands of miles away. The fragile butterfly can alter a weather pattern in another state; another continent.[10]

Based in the scientific chaos theory, scientists have learned that the flapping of those tiny butterfly wings causes a chain of events leading to large-scale alterations of weather patterns. Had the butterfly not flapped its wings, the trajectory of the weather system might have been vastly different. While a butterfly flapping its wings does not cause the tornado, it is an essential part of the initial conditions resulting in a violent storm hundreds of miles away.[11]

What lesson can you learn from this *butterfly effect*? You may feel as insignificant at times as the fragile butterfly. It may seem like you are just *flapping your wings* while standing alone for truth and honesty in your workplace or your home. You might feel foolish, even frightened at the consequences. You feel as if you are just making an insignificant, hardly noticeable, *flapping* movement against tremendous odds.

Yet, in the grand scheme of things, your "flapping wings" are initiating changes that will influence lives around you for all eternity. Standing for your smallest convictions has huge consequences for you and for others. They can defeat the enemy's purpose for your life and release God's purposes to become a reality. Don't be afraid to engage in the *butterfly effect*.

YOU DON'T HAVE TO FEAR THE LION

Winston Churchill was known for his exceedingly practical wisdom. Leading Britain through the dark days of World War II, he challenged his nation not to fear:

> One ought never to turn one's back on a threatened danger and try to run away from it. If you do that, you will double the danger. But if you meet it promptly and without flinching, you will reduce the danger by half. Never run away from anything. Never![12]

One of my favorite Bible heroes is a man named Benaiah, who did not turn his back on danger. In fact, he pursued a lion, which is one of the most dangerous animals you can ever encounter. Known as the king of beasts because of their great strength, male lions can measure more than eight feet in length, not counting the tail.

These flesh eaters have thirty sharp, piercing teeth, canines to grab and kill prey and scissorlike molars to slice into flesh. And they are capable of high speed for short distances, especially when attacking fleet-footed prey.[13]

Benaiah was the son of a valiant warrior, Jehoiada (2 Sam. 23).

It seems that the courage of his father had influenced Benaiah to become a fearless warrior also. On a snowy day, Benaiah decided to pursue a lion, knowing that he would have to kill it or be killed in the encounter.

The Bible tells us the outcome of that encounter but not the details. It says that Benaiah jumped into a pit where the lion was and killed it. He was tracking the lion; the lion was not stalking him. Evidently, he was alone. He had to rely on his courage to deliver him from a terrible death such as only a lion can inflict.

FEAR FIGHTER

A fear fighter takes risks against all odds.

To be a fear fighter you can't just be an average joe. You have to have the courage to take risks against all odds. You have to be like Benaiah and pursue your *lion* that poses a threat to you and your family.

That lion was an opportunity for Benaiah. Did he know that conquering that lion would become a part of his résumé? That it would open a door for his becoming one of David's mighty men? Probably not. Yet, he pursued it just the same.

And after becoming King David's bodyguard, Benaiah was later promoted to be the captain of the host of all of Israel under King Solomon. He became the second most powerful man in Israel because of the fearless courage he displayed. Each dangerous situation Benaiah faced was God's opportunity for him to become a victorious fear fighter.

Fear fighters take advantage of opportunities. They don't wait to be attacked; they go on the offensive when opportunity presents itself. God wants you to take advantage of your opportunities. If you sing, join the choir. If you are thinking about starting a new business, take the steps to investigate your possibilities. If you are lonely, make the effort to develop friendships.

It may seem like your scariest moment. I understand how you feel. But God loves to see you move out in faith and conquer your fears. When I said yes to that first opportunity to preach in my brother's revival service, I walked into that pulpit feeling scared and feeble.

I didn't know then that my fragile *flapping wings* were changing the spiritual weather patterns of my life. And I didn't dream that one little sermon would begin to blow change to the lives of a church in Gainesville, Georgia, to another church in Orange County, California, and to the nations of the world.

Look for and embrace the smallest opportunities God gives you. Pray and ask God to speak to you and show you what He wants you to do. When God is with you, He changes the *odds*. When God is in the equation, your nothingness plus God's almightiness equals more than enough.

Declare His Word: "I can do all things through Christ who strengthens me" (Phil. 4:13). Then, even if all you have is a *maybe*, you will be able to conquer your fear to step out in faith on that alone.

What to Do When All You Have Is a Maybe

Do you like to have a sure thing before you take a risk? Do you want to invest your money in something that guarantees a certain rate of return? Do you have to know that someone likes you before offering your friendship? Many times when God wants you to do something, it does not seem like a sure thing at first. Most of the great miracles in the Bible happened when people stepped out in faith on a *maybe*.

On one occasion, Jonathan, the son of King Saul, was pursuing the great Philistine army. I was struck by what he said to his armor bearer. He did not say he had a word from the Lord and he knew they were going to win the battle. Jonathan simply said to him, "Come, let us go over to the garrison of these uncircumcised; **it may be that the LORD will work for us.**" (1 Sam. 14:6, emphasis added). *Maybe* the Lord will help them? And if He did not, what then? Doesn't sound like a risk-free proposition.

Jonathan had faith that God was with him. He thought He might fight with him against these enemies of Israel. Still, he was not sure what would happen in that confrontation. So he said, "It may be..." Jonathan and his armor bearer risked their lives in faith with just a maybe.

As they showed themselves to the Philistines, they began to fight a few of them in an open field, slaughtering about twenty men. The Lord was with Jonathan and caused the entire Philistine army to erupt in great confusion. They began to kill each other and to flee before these two warriors who had dared to trust God with their *maybe*.

The trap of waiting for a sure thing

Always remember that courage is not the absence of fear; it's the mastery of fear. You have to master the fear of uncertainty. King Solomon, the wisest man who ever lived, said, "He who observes the wind will not sow, and he who regards the clouds will not reap" (Eccles. 11:4).

Solomon was saying that you have to take a chance sometimes even when it seems the *weather* is against you. Otherwise, you will never do anything worthwhile. It is better to sow seed and reap the harvest in spite of contrary winds and other uncertainties.

If you are like me, you want to wait to take a risk until conditions are perfect and you are absolutely sure that you will succeed. You want to know what the *clouds* are going to do and the effect of the *wind* on your endeavor.

I don't always have a sermon that I am absolutely certain is the Word of the Lord for that moment every time I step into the pulpit to preach. Sometimes I'm *iffy* about what the Lord wants me to preach. Many times when I have preached the *maybe* message I had prepared, the Lord worked mightily in the hearts and lives of believers and unbelievers alike.

It would be wonderful if God would send you a fax from heaven or an angel to thump you on the head to give you the divine direction. More often, God speaks in a still, small voice or an impression that you receive in prayer or when reading the Word. He might give you an idea when you are listening to someone preach or are reading the newspaper. That idea or impression begins to grow inside, and you wonder if it could be God—*maybe* He wants you to do this.

We like the guaranteed outcome. We are comfortable with the certain, absolute deal, with no risk of failure or loss. But the truth is, we are going to face a maybe more times than we will have guarantees. It is those times of uncertainty that try our resolve, prove our faith, and test our courage.

Your faith and courage are strengthened more readily when you have to live cautiously or when you explore a maybe as you meditate on His Word and submit yourself to the lordship of Christ. You may not be comfortable with this level of dependency on God. Your mind and carnal desire are to have the clear understanding of a *sure thing*. But faith in God's maybe is a safe place. God can turn your maybe into a miracle.

I am not talking about being presumptuous or pressing for your own personal desires. Sometimes when we want something to happen, we presume that God does too. When you feel like God is saying something to you, especially if it involves a major decision, you should seek the counsel of your pastor or other spiritual leaders in your life.

I never make a major decision in life without allowing two or three spiritual leaders to confirm it. That is a biblical principle for seeking godly counsel. I ask them to pray about it and see if God tells them something contrary.

After seeking counsel, ask yourself: "Is my motive right? Do I want only to do God's will?" Then you can say with confidence: "It may be the Lord is with me."

I have watched God work miracles for me many times when I was willing to seek Him and move out in faith on a maybe. My motive was right; I was praying and studying and waiting on

God. I sought counsel and then moved in faith against all odds. And God transformed my maybe into a miracle.

The secret to tapping into the *supernatural* is for you to have the courage to do the *natural* first. Jonathan knew he was no match for the Philistine army, but he courageously faced them with a maybe that the Lord would be with him. Without his action, God could not move in and change his maybe into a miracle.

What are your options?

Consider your options. If you are in a financial struggle, will you cave in to fear and let failure win? Will you let your dream for starting a business die inside you because of the risk involved? Is that potential relationship too scary to pursue? Will you compromise your godly convictions to please your children?

Don't wait for guarantees. Don't sit still and do nothing because your actions may carry a risk. Don't fear natural circumstances, obstacles, or frightening situations. Take the maybe you have been given, and begin to act on it. You will begin to see the hand of God turn it into a miracle if you refuse to give into fear.

If you are willing to face off with the fear of failure that has held you back from fulfilling your divine destiny, I encourage you to pray this prayer with me:

> *Dear Lord Jesus, help me to define failure and success as You do and not as the world does. Let me pursue the success You have ordained for my sake, for the sake of others, for Your sake, and for the enemy's sake. Let me have strength to step out on a maybe that You give me*

and pursue the lion that threatens my dream. Help me not to compromise my smallest convictions. Thank You for setting me free from the fear of failure. Let me grow in faith and benefit from times when I fail. And let me experience Your miracle in my maybe situation. Amen.

FEAR FIGHTER'S ARSENAL

Fighting the Fear of Failure

Be strong and of good courage; do not be afraid, nor be dismayed, for the LORD your God is with you wherever you go.

—JOSHUA 1:9

Wait on the LORD;
Be of good courage,
And He shall strengthen your heart;
Wait, I say, on the LORD.

—PSALM 27:14

Fear not…I will help you, says the LORD
And your Redeemer, the Holy One of Israel.

—ISAIAH 41:14

Do not fear, for you will not be ashamed;
Neither be disgraced, for you will not be put to shame…

—ISAIAH 54:4

My Personal Fear Fighters

_____

_____

_____

_____

_____

_____

_____

_____

_____

_____

_____

_____

_____

_____

_____

_____

_____

_____

8

OVERCOMING THE FEAR OF PEOPLE

HAVE YOU EVER felt awkward when you were invited to eat out with two or three couples, and you were alone? Did your parents or your boss, or other important persons in your life ever make you feel insignificant, *less than*, even worthless? How do you handle rejection? What do you do with your fear of people?

God called Jeremiah as a young man to be a prophet. Jeremiah protested that he was young and could not speak. Then

159

God told him that he would go wherever He sent him and speak whatever He told him to speak. And God said, "Do not be afraid of their faces, for I am with you to deliver you" (Jer. 1:8). He addressed Jeremiah's fear of people and promised to deliver him.

I wonder how many potential relationships have been thwarted because of a fear of people. This *learned* fear is one of the most detrimental to building marriages, friendships, and strong relationships. I shared with you how timid I was when I was a young man. Unless God had helped me to overcome my fear, I would not have enjoyed the wonderful marriage I have or many other vital relationships that have impacted my life.

If relationships of any kind spark anxiety and fear in your heart, I have good news for you. Jesus wants to set you free to experience meaningful relationships. I want you to pay close attention to the lesson He taught about the *fifth sparrow*.

There is no rejection in His love, only complete acceptance. There is no condemnation, just forgiveness and mercy.

He wanted people to know the love of God, so He taught them the great value that He puts on every individual life. As usual, He started His teaching by asking them about something they were very familiar with—*roasted sparrows*.

In those days, vendors carried on commerce in the open market by setting up small booths along the streets. Some vendors sold sparrows on a stick that they had roasted over an open fire. (They did not have McDonald's in those days; they had *McSparrow's*.)

Jesus said you could buy two of those roasted sparrows for one copper coin. But in some places, according to Jesus, you could get *five* sparrows for two copper coins. Obviously, shrewd vendors threw in a fifth sparrow for free.

FEAR FIGHTER

Receiving the love of Jesus is the first step to overcoming fear of rejection.

Third-grade math tells you that if two sparrows are sold for one copper coin, you should be able to buy four sparrows for two copper coins. But Jesus knew you could buy five sparrows for two small coins. That meant the fifth sparrow was worthless. It really had no value for the vendor. That fifth sparrow could be called the *odd bird out*.

Then Jesus told the people that not one sparrow falls to the ground without God noticing it. That would include even the *worthless* fifth sparrow. And Jesus said, "Do not fear therefore; you are of more value than many sparrows" (Luke 12:7).

EVER FELT THE SHAME OF BEING A *FALLEN ONE*?

Jesus also told the people that God knew each one of them so well that He even knew the number of all the hairs on their heads. What an awesome thought! If some of your hairs fell out this morning, God recalculated that number a few hours ago. (Of course, He has to do less calculation on some people than on others.) Someone said that old men don't go bald; their hair just goes underground and comes out of their noses and ears.

With such awesome knowledge of every individual, Jesus wanted them to be convinced that they did not have to be afraid; they were safe in God's love. He is saying the same to you today. Have you ever felt as worthless as that fifth sparrow? In tough times, life can tell you that you are nobody, headed nowhere. But Jesus does not want anyone to feel like a fifth sparrow. You are of great worth to God.

Regardless of what life has dealt to you that makes you feel *less than*, God still says you matter to Him. He sees great value in you. If you can believe that, you will have the power to conquer the fear of rejection. When you know how valuable you are to God, you will not fear what others think of you.

Jesus urged us over and over in Scripture to observe the fowl of the air. Apparently, He wants us to become bird watchers. He wants us to learn valuable spiritual lessons from the birds. But not just any birds...He mentioned sparrows specifically. He focused on these little birds that even today are considered common and insignificant among the bird community.

He didn't say to observe the strutting peacock. I learned a long time ago that a strutting peacock today can be tomorrow's feather duster. You need to be careful when you start strutting around in pride because of the blessing of God.

Don't ever forget where you came from. Remember what life was like before you knew Christ. And stay humble before the Lord in gratitude for what He has given you. The Lord values your humility and loathes your pride.

Jesus didn't specifically mention the beautiful cardinal or the noisy blue jay, or any other exotic bird we consider more valuable. He asked us to think about the common little sparrow. He told the people that little bird mattered to God. And He also told them they were of much more value than many sparrows.

God says that to you also. Do you know how valuable you are to God? He created you in His image. His whole purpose was for you to live in perfect fellowship with Him, not only in this life, but forever. And through Christ's death on Calvary, He bought you back to Himself to enjoy that communion with Him.

There are no fifth sparrows in God's mind. In fact, He is aware of every one of those little birds that falls to the ground. How much more is He aware of you? God says that even though people may not see value in you, He does. You are very valuable to Him.

Did you catch what Jesus said about those sparrows falling to the ground? God attends their funerals. I have never been to a sparrow's funeral, but He never misses one. God's great loving heart cares even for a sparrow that falls.

He knows what makes you feel worthless. When you wonder if you have any value or contribution to make to life…when you are falling to the ground in a quiet despair of worthlessness, God is there. You may think no one even knows you exist. But if God goes to the funeral of a fallen sparrow, He knows and cares about you, even when you mess up.

God is dealing with us as "fallen ones." Jesus's message is for people who were soaring at one time in life, but something happened, and you failed. Or someone devastated your self-worth, making you feel rejected. You became afraid and began to feel like a fifth sparrow, like you don't fit; you are the odd bird out without value or worth.

God wants you to know that if He would go to the funeral of a fallen sparrow, He cares about you when you fall and mess up. You are of great value in God's equation of love and grace! In short, there are no *fifth sparrows* with God—every person has great value in God's perspective. You count with Him. You are somebody to Him. And even when people don't put any worth in you anymore, God will never give up on you.

Self-exaltation leads to pride, which God hates. But self-deprecation leads to paralysis. It creates a terrible atmosphere where fear prevails. Neither attitude is pleasing to God. The devil has made a lot of people feel as if they are not worth anything...that they are just a big failure, and their lives are one big mistake after another.

If you believe his lie, you let life paint you into the picture of a fifth sparrow that is worthless, that doesn't fit in. Other people have value; they succeed. But whatever has happened in your life makes you feel as though you are less than other people.

You need to know that Jesus displayed your great value to Him when He hung on a cross at Calvary. He loved you personally so much that He was willing to lay down His life for you so that you could be free to be the person He made you to be. And He told you not to be afraid that you have failed God so much that He doesn't love you anymore.

I don't care how many times you have tried and failed. God's message to you is that He still loves you. The smallest detail of your life does not escape God's gaze. He still sees worth in you. He knows your potential. And He has a plan and purpose for your life. His love for you is special. It's like God has your picture on His refrigerator.

Do You Feel Like the *Odd Bird Out?*

I think everyone faces the fear at some time of being the *odd bird out*, of standing alone without the approval of others. You may be in a season of feeling like you are not as special or valuable as other members of your family or your friends—or even of your brothers and sisters in Christ. There were people in the Bible who were considered odd birds by others. The Bible tells us how God thinks about them.

> **FEAR** FIGHTER
>
> To God, you count. You are somebody.

David was the odd bird. He was treated like the fifth sparrow of the family. Do you remember when Samuel was sent to the house of Jesse, David's father, to anoint the next king of Israel? They had a big banquet, and then it came time to anoint one of his seven sons who were present. Samuel looked at each one and admired them for their physical appearance.

Their father would recommend each one to Samuel as they passed before him. "This boy is handsome. This boy has real talent. This one is very intelligent. I think this one would make an excellent king!"

But God spoke to Samuel that He had refused all of these sons. He told him that He does not see as man sees; man looks at the outward appearance, but He looks at the heart (1 Sam. 16:7). So Samuel asked Jesse if he had any other sons.

Jesse said his youngest son was in the field keeping the sheep. His daddy had not even invited him to the feast. He was just the youngest son, not yet worth much to his family. His father did not even consider presenting him to the prophet. He was like the fifth sparrow that did not have any value among his peers.

I have learned something about God. He often passes over the *hotshots* and picks from the back of the line. God loves to choose people whom others pass over, reject, and put down. They predict: "He or she will never amount to anything."

But if you let God put His hand on you, He will choose you over the hotshots. He looks at your heart and says: "I can use him." "I can use her." When you humble yourself under the mighty hand of God, He will exalt you in due time (1 Pet. 5:6). Don't let anyone tell you that you are a fifth sparrow!

OVERCOMING THE FEAR OF ALONENESS

The psalmist expressed feelings of aloneness and dejection when he said, "I am like a pelican of the wilderness; I am like an owl of the desert…and am like a sparrow alone on the housetop" (Ps. 102:6–7). He felt like an odd bird, alone. What was the scene he was watching?

Maybe the sparrow's nest had been torn apart. Maybe he had lost his family in a storm or to a beast of prey. Maybe his mate had died. For whatever reason, the sparrow was alone and lonely.

Even Jesus knew what it meant to be alone without people who understood Him. His disciples did not understand Him.

They were concerned about which of them was the greatest. They could not even pray with Him in His most difficult moments. And on the cross He cried out, "My God, my God, why hast thou forsaken me?" (Matt. 27:46, KJV).

Aloneness can do a number on your sense of worth. Some of you, through death of your spouse or divorce or other painful circumstances, are walking through a season where you feel like the odd bird. You don't have anyone who really understands what you are going through. Life has dealt you a blow that has made you feel less than.

Recently, my wife and I took a cruise. We noticed people who sat alone during the entire cruise. They ate every meal alone. And our hearts were touched by their aloneness. I remembered that as a single young man, even when I was in a crowd I could feel lonely.

Everyone faces times of aloneness and loneliness. The good news is that even if your relationships are in trouble, the Lord wants you to know that He will never leave you alone or forsake you (Heb. 13:5). He will be there for you. He will never abandon you. You don't have to be afraid of being alone the rest of your life. He will show you the way out of your pain and loneliness.

I understand the fear that grips young people in their twenties who wonder if they will ever find the right person to marry. For every person who has a desire for marriage, I believe you can trust God that your perfect mate is living and breathing somewhere on the planet. God has the greatest dating service in the world. It is better than "Find a Mate.com." If you will seek God first and decide to serve Him with all your heart, He will move heaven and Earth to cross your paths with that special person.

If you are widowed, single, divorced, or have never married and you want to find marital happiness, don't be anxious. God is in control of your love life if you submit your life to Him. Your steps are ordered of the Lord. It is exciting to watch the future unfold when you place your confidence in His goodness and His plan for your life. God has opportunities for you that you have never dreamed possible.

My mother's story

My dad had a heart attack and died suddenly at the age of fifty-six. My mother was a young widow, left alone with my sixteen-year-old sister, Jill. The small inheritance Dad had left lasted only a couple of years. Then, they began to experience financial need. All my mom had ever known was the life of a minister's wife and homemaker.

She is not the type of person who would talk about her situation to anyone, not even to me or my brothers and sisters. Instead, she determined to seek the Lord in fasting and prayer. She gave herself to pray and fast for three days, as Queen Esther of old had done.

Mom had no idea what she was going to do to make it through those tough times. One day during her fast, she prayed: "Lord, if You will direct my steps, I will go anywhere and do whatever You want me to do. I will work a secular job and witness for You by my lifestyle. I will take a position in a church or ministry. As long as I know You are leading me, I will do whatever You want me to do."

When she finished praying that prayer, she laid her head down to rest. Not five minutes later, her telephone rang. When she answered the phone, she heard the voice of my wife, Cherise. My wife didn't greet her in a normal way with "hello" or any small talk. She came straight to the point and said, "Well, you might as well pack your things because you're coming. Here's Jentezen."

FEAR FIGHTER

The Lord will never leave you
alone or forsake you.

Of course, I had no clue that Mom had been praying about direction for her life; all I knew was that I needed help. I got on the phone and said, "Mom I've been asking you for two years to come and help me. The church is growing so fast that I don't have time to pray and study like I should while I'm just trying to keep up with everything. I need you to help me with hospital visits and to love the people. I need you to do for me what you did for Daddy's ministry. If you don't come, I'm going to hire someone else, so I need you to tell me now if you're coming."

My mom began to give me all kinds of excuses. Her life had been wrapped up in my dad's ministry, and she still had trouble making decisions sometimes. She never had to make a big decision like this one on her own. While she continued with her excuses, the Lord reminded her of what she had just prayed moments earlier: "I will do whatever You want me to do."

Mom finally said yes, and on September 2, 1993, she moved to Gainesville, Georgia, to become a part of my staff at Free Chapel.

Now, sixteen years later, Mom is one of the most loved and active members of my staff. She and her loyal volunteers visit six rest homes each week. They bring those precious people a message of hope and brighten their day with music.

Mom also leads our convalescent care ministry, which offers wonderful home-cooked meals to comfort families who have lost loved ones. Because of the demands of the ministry, I rarely have an opportunity to make hospital visits. I often joke with the congregation that they would rather have my mom come by and visit than me, because if I come it might mean something bad is happening.

I love to tell this amusing but true story to emphasize the importance of Mom's ministry at Free Chapel. My wife and I were visiting my sister-in-law at the hospital just after she had a baby. My wife heard that an elderly lady from the church was also in the hospital and told me that I should go to see her. So, I went by her room, and as I entered the door, the lady sat up in the bed abruptly.

Her countenance was distorted, as though she had seen a ghost! She began to say, "Oh no, they didn't tell me it was *that bad*!" She thought she must have a terminal condition because I had come to visit and pray with her instead of my mother. I felt as though I was the death angel! I had to reassure her that my being there did not mean there was bad news.

Whenever our members have a serious need and call the church for prayer, they don't ask for me; they ask for my mom. She is absolutely vital to the ministry, and our entire congregation values her immensely. She dared to leave her home and all that was familiar to become a part of the ministry at Free Chapel.

Her loving surrender to obedience to the Lord opened for her an amazing opportunity for life-giving ministry.

God knows your aloneness just as He knew my mother's. He knows that you can be extremely useful and fruitful in His kingdom if you will determine to overcome your fear and seek Him for His divine opportunities.

JESUS SEEKS OUT THE LONELY

Jesus typically sought out the people who were alone in a crowd. He called His disciples individually to follow Him. And He had an appointment with a solitary Samaritan woman who came to a well to draw water. He offered her living water that changed her life. He offered the man at the pool of Bethesda the cure he could not receive otherwise, because he had no one to help him get into the water.

After His resurrection, Jesus did not go to Rome or Athens or any other metropolis. There is no record that He visited the multitudes. He revealed Himself to a lonely, grief-stricken woman outside the tomb. When He called her name, "Mary," she knew His voice. He walked with two troubled men on the road to Emmaus, and they recognized Him when He broke bread with them. And He appeared to His disciples hiding in fear behind closed doors.

Jesus was constantly reaching out to the down-and-outers, the lonely, the odd birds. If that is how you feel, then you can expect to have a special audience with the Lord. He wants to spend time with you to tell you that you don't have to be afraid of aloneness.

You are not alone when Christ is with you. He does not consider you a fifth sparrow. He sees you when you fall. Why? Because He cares about every detail of your life.

God has a plan for your life, and He wants you to walk with Him to fulfill it—together. His promise to you is: "For I know the thoughts that I think toward you, says the LORD, thoughts of peace and not of evil, to give you a future and a hope" (Jer. 29:11).

No matter how great your failure, He has a plan for your life filled with hope and not despair. I dare you to declare: "God only thinks good things about me and plans good things for me." It is true, because He loves you with an everlasting love—a love that made Him lay down His life for you. He will never reject you or leave you alone. In that reality, you can have hope to overcome those fears. The psalmist declared that God's thoughts toward him were precious and were so many that he could not count them (Ps. 139: 18).

You have a home in God, in His heart, and in His thoughts. There is a place even for the insignificant sparrow to dwell in the presence of God. The psalmist said that the sparrow had found a house for herself where she could raise her young in the altars of God (Ps. 84:3).

He allowed the most insignificant fifth sparrow to dwell in His presence. She was safe to build her nest and raise her family in that place of worship, the holy tabernacle. That is a beautiful picture of your safe place in the presence of God. As you bow in worship, He will lift you up and make you feel valuable and safe. He will deliver you from fear of rejection and aloneness.

You can't hide *from* God, but you can hide *in* God. You can *nest* in His safety and in His protection, blessing, and presence. You can never feel alone or afraid in His presence. No matter what life throws your way, you don't have to feel like you are less than. You are important to God. His love will always be there for you even in seasons of trouble and loss.

Never Alone in Adversity

I thought about Job, who was one of the wealthiest men of his time. The Bible says he feared God and hated evil. Yet, in one day the bottom dropped out of his life. He lost his wealth, his children, and his health and was betrayed by his wife. She told him to curse God and die. Then, four of his friends came and sat around him where he was on the ash heap.

For seven days they just sat there, not saying a word, just looking at him with an accusing look. He sat there, the *fifth sparrow* in the middle of those four friends. They were there to tell him how he had failed God. They wanted him to confess the sin that had caused all this calamity. They accused him of messing up. Their long speeches told him all the reasons they knew he was not the righteous man he claimed to be.

What did Job do? He had to decide how he was going to face his adversity. He could not deny the bad news. Everything that he valued in life had been lost. But he settled it in his heart. He would not accuse God or feel sorry for himself. He simply declared: "The Lord gave, and the Lord hath taken away; blessed be the name of the Lord" (Job 1:21, kjv). He knew the greatest thing in life was the presence of the Lord. Job chose to bless the name of the Lord in his painful aloneness.

When his wife told him to curse God and die, Job said, "No,

thank you. I will bless the name of the Lord and live! I still have His presence! I don't understand why all this is happening, but I know that He is with me." And the Bible says that God restored to Job twice as much as he had in the beginning.

What have you lost? Are you tempted to blame God for your painful situation? I encourage you to do like Job and bless the name of the Lord. He is with you in your pain, and He can turn your weeping into joy once again. He wants to give you a safe place to dwell in His presence continually. You are not alone. You don't have to be afraid in your adversity.

Do you feel like you have failed miserably and that there is no future for you? If you take failure personally, you will also take success personally. You need to give your failures and your successes to God. You can't go back and start over, but you can start again and make a brand-new end. Today is the first day of the rest of your life!

MASTER OR MASCOT?

It became obvious to all that God was truly Job's Master. In the cruelest adversity, Job honored Him as his God. He chose to bless the name of the Lord. That is the key to overcoming fear of the future or any other fear.

God takes failures and redeems them by His blood. He takes what the world says is worthless and reveals the great value He has placed in you. But He demands to be Master and Lord of your life. That is His rightful place. A lot of people want God to take their sin and guilt and let them enjoy their freedom. But then they treat Him as their *mascot* and not their Master.

Do you know what a mascot is? It's like the University of Georgia's bulldog. During halftime of a football game, they take that bulldog out of the cage and run him across the field. Everybody hoops and hollers for their mascot. Then, they put him back in the cage and leave him there until next week's game.

That's what a lot of Christians do with Jesus. They come to church one day a week and get excited in the presence of the Lord. Then they live the rest of the week without thinking about Him. And Jesus says, "You don't talk to Me. You don't listen to Me. You don't read My Word. I want to be Master on Monday, Tuesday, Wednesday, Thursday, Friday, and Saturday. I'm not a mascot to applaud on Sunday. I am your Master. And if you will give Me your life, I will do something with it!"

> ## FEAR FIGHTER
> God only thinks good things about me and plans good things for me.

The devil wants you to feel like a fifth sparrow—worthless, odd, and insignificant. God wants to make your life significant. He wants to develop all the potential He placed inside of you to contribute to His purposes in the earth. You will not feel insignificant if you will make Him Lord and Master of your life.

FREE FROM SHAME

I love this true story about an odd bird who came to know God
as His Master. A seminary professor and his family were vaca-
tioning in the hills of Tennessee. They stopped in a little country
town in East Tennessee to eat a meal in a local diner there. When
they were seated, they ordered their meal.

As they were served, they noticed an old man going from
table to table talking to the customers. The professor cringed at
the thought that the man might come to their table. He wished
he would just leave them alone. But sooner than he would have
liked, the old man came to talk to them.

> "How ya'll doin?' he asked. Then without waiting for
> an answer: "Ya'll not from these parts, are ya?"
> "No."
> "Well, where ya'll from, and what do ya do?"
> "We are from Oklahoma, and I am a seminary
> professor."
> "Oh, really? So, you teach preachers how to preach,
> do ya? Ya know, I once knew a pastor who impacted
> my life in such a way that it changed me forever." The
> old man was gaining interest in his recollection.
> "How do you mean?" asked the professor, trying to
> be polite as he took another bite of his meal.
> "Well, I've grown up in these parts of East Tennessee
> all my life. This is a very small community. Everybody
> knows everybody and everybody's business. So, every-
> body knows I never knew who my father was. I was
> illegitimate. Everywhere I went, it seemed someone

was taunting me with the question, 'Who is your daddy?'"

He continued, thoughtfully, "All my life I felt less than others, you know. I felt odd. When I played ball, all the other kids had a dad at the game. All I ever had was my mother and grandmother. And somehow I felt ashamed. In public, I sat in the corner. I isolated myself from others. I felt inferior because I did not have a father."

The old man's eyes glistened as he said, "Then, one day, my grandmother started taking me to church. I will never forget it. I started listening to what that preacher was sayin.' And one Sunday, when we was leavin,' the preacher was at the door shaking hands with the people. As I went by, he shook my hand. Then he bent over and whispered something in my ear."

Now, the old man was wiping tears, unashamed, before he went on with his story. "He whispered in my ear, 'Son, I know who your father is. Your father is God. And He's the best Father that any person could ever have. And don't you let anyone tell you any different.'"

Then the old man looked the professor right in the eye and said, "I can't explain it, but something clicked inside of me that day. A light came on. I began to see God as my own Father. And you know what? God has been very good to me."

With that, the old man left their table and walked out of the diner. When the professor and his family finished eating, he went to the cash register and asked,

"You know that old man who was walking around talking to everyone?"

"Yeah."

"Well, who is he? And what is his deal?" queried the professor, trying to hide his sarcasm.

"You don't know?" asked the man behind the cash register, incredulously. "Why, that is Ben Hooper. He is the former two-term governor of Tennessee [1910–1914)]. And he has done more good for this community and this entire state than anyone I know. He is an amazing man!"[1]

That's what can happen when you realize that you are not a fifth sparrow. You don't have to live in shame because of what your mother or father did. Or because of what you have done. Somebody had to tell Ben Hooper that he was of great value to God, that God was his heavenly Father. Ben had to know that just because he was taunted as an *illegitimate* son, it didn't mean that he had no value. In fact, the Bible says that God is a "father of the fatherless" (Ps. 68:5).

God spoke to my heart to tell every fatherless child who has been abandoned by their dad that God may have trusted your father to carry your seed, but He did not trust him to carry you through life, to raise you and teach you the ways of God. The psalmist said, "When my father and my mother forsake me, then the LORD will take care of me" (Ps. 27:10).

If God allowed you to be separated from your biological father, perhaps He knew that you would not have connected with His plan otherwise. If you make Christ the Master of your life, you can know the same kind of loving care that Ben Hooper discovered.

Ben Hooper's pastor knew that day that he was talking to a hurting little boy who needed to know who his father was. He needed to know that God was the best Father anyone could have. God showed Ben Hooper how much He loved him, how valuable and special he was. He was not a fifth sparrow. He was of great worth to his Father. And, in turn, he was able to bless thousands of lives by becoming all God meant for him to be.

You don't have to fear aloneness, because you are never alone. And you don't have to fear relationships, because God gives grace to love others and to forgive. He teaches you how to show mercy and to enjoy the love and fellowship He provides.

Some of you feel like the fifth sparrow sold on that skewer for pennies. Life has stuck it to you and roasted you. You feel worthless in life. That is a lie from the devil. God does not have any fifth sparrows in His economy. He loves you, and He has a plan for your life. God has a place for you and a purpose that will bring fulfillment and satisfaction to your life.

You simply have to answer this question, "Is He Master or mascot? Does He sit on the throne of your heart?" When that issue is settled, you will begin to know His love and be set free from fear of aloneness and rejection.

Jesus built a whole doctrine on the *eradication of fear* based on the value of one sparrow. And He commanded, "Do not fear therefore; you are of more value than many sparrows" (Luke 12:7). If you want to ask God to set you free from these fears and from any sense of shame, pray this prayer with me:

Dear Lord Jesus, I come to make You Master of my life. I want to submit to Your lordship and find Your purpose for my life. I break the fear of rejection and aloneness over my life, in the name of Jesus. I declare that I am free from shame as a child of God. And I thank You, Lord, for Your power working in my life to give me a future and a hope. Thank You for the relationships You have for me. You will give me all I need in friends and family. I confess that I will not be alone, because You are with me. And Your love for me is setting me free from fear and shame. Thank You, Jesus. I love You.

FEAR FIGHTER'S ARSENAL

Overcoming the Fear of People

The LORD is on my side;
I will not fear.
What can man do to me?

—PSALM 118:6

For I know the thoughts that I think toward you, says the
LORD, thoughts of peace and not of evil, to give you a future
and a hope.

—JEREMIAH 29:11

Do not fear, little flock, for it is your Father's good pleasure
to give you the kingdom.

—LUKE 12:32

Lo I am with you always, even to the end of the age.

—MATTHEW 28:20

For He Himself has said, "I will never leave you nor forsake
you." So we may boldly say: "The LORD is my helper; I will
not fear. What can man do to me?"

—HEBREWS 13:5

My Personal Fear Fighters

_____

_____

_____

_____

_____

_____

_____

_____

_____

_____

_____

_____

_____

_____

_____

_____

_____

_____

9

NO FEAR OF ETERNITY

EATH STALKS US all. It is a formidable foe. We can try to ignore it, but the ball and chain of death sooner or later yanks us all back into reality. At first when we are born we are fragile. Then for a *moment* we are strong. Sometimes we are tricked by the resilience of our youth into ignoring our mortality until finally, without fail, we all find the canker of disease gnawing somewhere inside our body. In the end, we are frail again—and we die.

Given free rein, the black giant of death would have long since sent this planet hurling through space like an abandoned ship. But in a stable yard at Bethlehem, within earshot of the lowing oxen and under the brilliance of a flaming star, through a teenage peasant girl the antagonist for death was born! Death had reigned supreme for six thousand years, but Jesus conquered it in three days! Rattling the keys of death and hell, Jesus rose on the third day saying, "I am He who lives, and was dead, and behold, I am alive forevermore" (Rev. 1:18).

A legend is told of a missionary in Brazil who discovered a tribe of natives living in a remote part of the jungle next to a large river. The natives were convinced that the river was filled with evil spirits, and consequently they were afraid to cross it. Disease was rampant among their population, and they were dying daily. They desperately needed medicine or the whole tribe would be wiped out. The only way to get help was to traverse that river they were terrified to cross.

The missionary explained to the tribe that the river was not haunted and was not evil. But it was to no avail. So he reached down into the river, splashing himself with the water, and saying to them again: "See, it's not evil. You don't have to be afraid to cross the river." But again, it was to no avail. So he waded out into the river and splashed around. Looking back at them, he signaled to them to come into the water. But his words fell on deaf ears.

The missionary was so consumed with compassion to see them made well and healed that in desperation he plunged into the black, angry river. He swam beneath the surface until he reached the other side and when he struggled up onto the shore, he thrust a triumphant fist into the air, facing the natives standing on the other side of the river. When he did that, there was a great shout that rose up and one after another of the tribesmen clambered into the water and began swimming across the river they had feared so much.

The missionary had to become an example of overcoming the terror of that river in order to set free the tribe who feared it. In that same way, Jesus Christ, through His death and resurrection, *swam the river* of our final foe called *death*. And He has come out triumphantly on the other side! We have nothing to fear! Christ has already made a pathway for us to safely cross over to the other side:

> Forasmuch then as the children are partakers of flesh and blood, he also himself likewise took part of the same; that through death he might destroy him that had the power of death, that is, the devil; and deliver them who through fear of death were all their lifetime subject to bondage.
>
> —Hebrews 2:14–15, kjv

Heaven is a place where every house is a mansion, every step is a march in unity, every meal is a banquet, every moment is ecstasy, every hour is rapture, and every day is jubilee. There will be no fevers, no exhausting pain, no hospitals filled with those waiting to die. There will be no sad good-byes.

Here on Earth we see mothers brushing back tears, and fathers, normally stoic and strong, who weep with broken hearts. We see the aged, with quiet resolve, bidding loved ones farewell. But the

Bible says that in heaven, "God will wipe away every tear from their eyes" (Rev. 7:17). It teaches that our last breath here will be our first breath there! And heaven is a place where we'll never say good-bye.

In fact, the Bible says that we cannot imagine how wonderful our life will be in heaven. Jesus told His disciples He was going to prepare a place for them so that they could be where He is (John 14: 2). And the apostle Paul said, "Eye has not seen, nor ear heard, nor have entered into the heart of man the things which God has prepared for those who love Him" (1 Cor. 2:9).

The only question that remains for you, personally, to answer is, Where will I go when I die? The Bible says there are two options for your future in eternity—a state of bliss in *heaven*, or eternal torment in *hell*. Of course, you can choose not to believe the Bible, which some believe would give you other apparent options. Or would it?

What if the Bible is true, and these are your only two options for living forever after death? That would mean you have a fifty-fifty chance of being right or wrong. What happens if you are wrong? If there is life after death...if heaven and hell are real...what will it be like for you? Should you be filled with dread or anticipation?

SHOULD *YOU* FEAR DEATH?

According to studies, most people admit to having some anxiety about death. Patterns of death anxiety show that:

- Women tend to report somewhat higher levels of death-related anxiety.

- Older people in general seem to have *less* death anxiety.

- People with mental and emotional disorders tend to suffer from a higher level of death anxiety.

- Death anxiety can spike temporarily to a higher level for people who have been exposed to traumatic situations.[1]

If you are like most people who do not want to think about death, what causes your greatest anxiety? Fear of a plane crash? A terrorist attack? Of falling from heights? If so, you are not alone. These are some of the most-feared causes of death. However, the likelihood of dying from these causes is remote. Here are the facts:

Likelihood of Most-Feared Causes of Death

• The actual risk of death in a plane crash would be once in 19,000 years if you flew on an airplane once a day for 19,000 years.
• Between the year 1580 and 2003 there have been 1,909 confirmed shark attacks. The real odds of being killed by a shark are zero in 264.1 million.
• Falling deaths are estimated to kill 80 people each year, mainly among those who work at heights in construction.
• Historically speaking, you have a one in 9.3 million chance of dying from a terrorist attack.
• Death from natural disaster is less likely than being killed by a fire or committing suicide.[2]

One thing is certain: everyone will die. Until Jesus returns as He has promised to do and takes believers to be with Him (1 Thess. 4:17), the only way to leave this world is by dying. The Bible teaches clearly that when that happens, you will face one of two fates: to live eternally in the presence of God, or to live eternally in hell with Satan.

Jesus taught plainly about heaven and hell and made it clear that one of those places would be your eternal destination. He warned:

> And I say to you, My friends, do not be afraid of those who kill the body, and after that have no more that they can do. But I will show you whom you should fear: fear Him who, after He has killed, has power to cast into hell; yes, I say to you, fear Him!
>
> —LUKE 12:4–5

This is the only time that Jesus told us to fear. After all the "fear nots" He gave to us, He made sure that we knew there was someone we must fear. It was His warning to us in order to avoid eternal damnation. *Eternal* means "forever, never-ending." The fact is that you will be alive thousands of years from now— somewhere. Should you fear the place where you will be?

HELL IS A PLACE

Hell is one of the most difficult subjects I have to deal with as a minister. I don't enjoy talking about hell. But when I read the words of Jesus, I am constantly reminded that there is a place called *hell*, and that it is a place of eternal torment. Jesus said the pathway to destruction was very broad and that many would go down that path (Matt. 7:13).

Most people refuse to think about death or eternity. They choose to simply live in denial. They don't think about what it would be like to spend forever in hell, where Jesus said the fire is never quenched (Mark 9:43). That is why Jesus talked so much about hell. He knew people would try to block it out of their minds. The devil would help them do just that by deceiving them, working hard to keep them from believing in Jesus or in hell.

Jesus taught that the justice of God demands a place be prepared for those who reject His sacrificial death on Calvary. He also said that hell was not prepared for people; it was prepared for the devil and his angels (Matt. 25:41). God does not want anyone to perish (2 Pet. 3:9). That is why Jesus came to die for our sin. Everyone who accepts His forgiveness for sin will escape hell and live in heaven with Him forever.

But it is the devil's goal to take as many people with him as possible into the lake of fire. He works to deceive them into rejecting the salvation that Jesus came to give to all who accept Him as Savior. He tries to get them not to believe in his existence and to mock those who do believe.

What is the atmosphere of hell?

What is the atmosphere in hell going to be like? That will be determined by the kind of people who go there. The Bible says that drunkards, adulterers, revelers, murderers, idolaters, sorcerers, liars, and every wicked person will be there (Gal. 5:19–21; Rev. 21:8). It is not a happy place. Even if hell wasn't a place of everlasting fire and torment, the inhabitants there would make the atmosphere intolerable.

Did you know that the word *sorcery* in the Greek is *pharmakeia,* which is the root form of pharmaceutical drugs? Our drug culture today that helps people escape life through addiction is leading them straight to hell. Every cocaine addict who snorts it up his nose…every teenager who smokes a joint…the heroin addict who shoots that needle into his vein…will find themselves one day burning in the lake of fire. Unless they repent and ask Jesus to deliver them from their addiction, they will know eternal torment. There will be no more escaping that reality.

> **FEAR** FIGHTER
>
> There is no escape from the
> reality of hell.

Are you a "reveler"? Do you live to party with your buddies? Are drinking and carousing your favorite pastimes? I believe there is a party spirit loose upon our nation that says: "Live for the moment; go for the gusto! You don't need God! Live for yourself!" According to the Bible, that lifestyle will also take you to hell.

Jesus described hell in a story of a rich man who enjoyed the good life and lived extravagantly and selfishly. There was a beggar named Lazarus who was laid at his gate, desiring only the crumbs that fell from the rich man's table. He was filled with sores and lived in misery. When the beggar died, the angels carried him to paradise to be with Abraham. After that, the rich man died. Jesus said he was in torment in the flames of Hades.

Then the rich man looked and saw Abraham a long way away, and he asked Abraham to let Lazarus just dip his finger in water and come to cool his tongue. Abraham said that he could not come to him because of the great gulf between them. The rich man wanted someone to go back and warn his five brothers so that they would not come to that place of torment (Luke 16:20–27). That was not possible either. Jesus made it clear from this story that hell is a very real *place*, and there is no escape from its torment.

Jesus lamented, "For what will it profit a man if he gains the whole world, and loses his own soul?" (Mark 8:36). It wasn't that riches in themselves were evil. But Jesus was saying that if you live for everything the world calls "gain," you could still lose your soul. You must choose to follow Christ on Earth in order to spend eternity with Him.

It is possible that PhDs, scientists, doctors, sports icons, music idols, and any other persons of notoriety could lose their souls. No one is exempt from eternal damnation unless they accept salvation provided through the blood of Christ. The Bible says that there is no salvation in any other name (Acts 4:12). Only submission to the lordship of Christ will allow you to escape the horrors of hell and assure you of eternal life in heaven with Him.

Jesus described hell with words like *destruction, damnation, outer darkness, torment,* and *everlasting fire.* Can you imagine living in darkness forever? Wishing for the day? Begging for relief from the flame? You cannot live wrong and die right!

If you are living wrong, you will die wrong and go to a place called hell. It is a place that is void of the presence of God. No light! No love! No peace! No joy! The Bible says that in hell there will be torment day and night, forever and ever (Rev. 20:10).

There are no exits from hell, no time off for good behavior. Once you are there, you have no way out. That is the choice you make when you are living your life on Earth. It is the dreadful outcome of rejecting Christ, and it takes you to a terrible place, a place called *hell*. Hell is no joke! Your friends can mock and laugh you *into* hell, but they can't laugh you out of hell.

The good news is that the Bible says if you repent and accept Christ as your Savior, God blots out all of your sin and does not even remember it (Isa. 43:25). In other words, God says that if you repent, He will *think* your sins out of existence. He accepts you as His forgiven son or daughter and gives you the privilege of living with Him forever. You exchange the terrible place called hell for the indescribably wonderful place called heaven.

HEAVEN IS A PLACE

Jesus taught that heaven is also a *place*. Jesus told His disciples He was going to prepare a place for them. He said that in His Father's house there are many mansions. And Jesus promised to take them there to be with Him forever (John 14:1–2).

What is heaven like? The atmosphere of heaven will be the essence of pure love, because God is love (1 John 4:16). It will be filled with light, because there is no darkness in Him. Peace, joy, and righteousness will reign in the light of His love.

The Bible gives us glimpses inside of heaven. On several occasions, the heavens open to allow people on Earth to see inside. When Jesus was baptized, the heavens were opened to Him, and He saw the Spirit of God descending like a dove and resting on Him (Matt. 3:16). When Stephen was stoned to death, he saw the heavens opened and Christ standing at the right hand of God (Acts 7:56).

Peter also saw heaven open when the Lord gave him a vision to teach him that salvation was for everyone (Acts 10:10–15). The apostle Paul was taken into the third heaven and shown divine secrets that he could not even share (2 Cor. 12:2–3). And the apostle John saw a door standing open in heaven when Jesus showed him things to come in the Book of Revelation (Rev. 4:1).

FEAR FIGHTER

If you repent, God will *think* your sins out of existence.

John saw the New Jerusalem, which is called *the City of God*. It could be called the *capital city* of heaven. John was permitted to measure it and found it is square and is fifteen hundred miles on each side and fifteen hundred miles tall. Its foundations are made of precious, transparent stones like sapphire, jasper, and sardonyx. The radiant sun of God's glory shines throughout that beautiful city, dazzling light reflecting through those stones.

The streets of heaven are paved with transparent gold. There is a pure river of water of life, clear as crystal, proceeding from the throne of God. Along the river is the tree of life filled with fruits. And the leaves of the tree were for the healing of the nations (Rev. 22:1–2). We know that there is a magnificent banquet hall in heaven where Jesus will eat the marriage supper of the Lamb with all of His sons and daughters.

These are just glimpses of the wonderful place called heaven, which is promised to all who serve Christ on the earth. It is a place of worship where the Lord of love dwells. And there will be no sorrow or tears there, for He will wipe away all tears. Eternal bliss, living forever with the giver of life, is the reward that awaits you in heaven.

Heaven's reward

We live such few years on Earth even if we live to be seventy or eighty or older. Compared to eternity that never ends, there is nothing we have to sacrifice here that is worth missing heaven. The apostle Paul said: "For to me, to live is Christ, and to die is gain" (Phil. 1:21). He seemed almost anxious to leave this world behind to live eternally with his Lord.

When the apostle Paul knew it was time for him to die he said:

> I have fought the good fight, I have finished the race, I have kept the faith. Finally, there is laid up for me the crown of righteousness, which the Lord, the righteous Judge, will give to me on that Day, and not to me only but also to all who have loved His appearing.
>
> —2 Timothy 4:7–8

It was obvious that Paul did not fear death. On the contrary, he was filled with anticipation. He knew he would be with his Lord and that he would receive his reward—a crown of righteousness. He declared his fight of faith was over, and he had overcome.

Promise of reward for overcomers

Jesus told the apostle John that he who overcomes will receive a white stone with a name written on it, which no one knows except the one who receives it (Rev. 2:17). Jesus was talking to the church in the city of Pergamos, which had honored His name even in the place where Satan's throne is (v. 13). Yet, some of them had compromised with the evil in that place, and He commanded them to repent. Then He promised that those who overcame would be rewarded—with a white stone.

Why a white stone? What kind of reward would that be? The people in Pergamos would have been very familiar with that term. There were several uses of the white stone that made it very significant to their lives.

Justification

The judicial system in that city had a special use for a white stone. When someone was accused of a crime, the defendant had to appear before a judge. The accuser would come and plead the case to the judge against him. After listening to both sides of the case, the judge would leave the courtyard for a time of deliberation. During that time the defendant was left standing in front of a pile of white stones with the people of the city standing around waiting for the judge's return.

When the judge walked back into the courtyard, every mouth was silenced and every eye was turned toward him. In his hand, the judge would either have a black stone, called the *stone of condemnation*, or a white stone, called the *stone of justification*.

If he handed the black stone to the defendant, the people of the city would pick up stones out of the pile and begin to stone him to death in the courtyard. But if he handed the accused one a white stone, it meant that all charges were dropped against him. The defendant was justified, found guiltless, and was to be released. They took off his chains and let him go free. He had been given the white stone of justification.[3]

Jesus promised a white stone to everyone who overcame the evil of their culture. Those who honored Christ and refused to compromise would be justified. And He personalized it. That white stone would have a name written on it that only the one who received it would know.

Someone has said that to be *justified* means to live in total freedom, "just-as-if-I'd never sinned." What a heavenly reward Jesus promises to every believer! When your sins are covered by the blood of Jesus you are justified, free from all guilt. As if you had never sinned! No more guilt! No more condemnation!

Victory

The white stone was also used in that culture to reward *victory*. When their armies came back from battle with another nation, the citizens of the city would line the streets to welcome home their war heroes. The king of the city would hand out white stones to the leaders in battle, which were equivalent to our medals of war.

Not everyone merits receiving a "white stone" medal, only those who fought the battle. That is a significant fact for every fear fighter. If you win the battle today, you will be promoted tomorrow. There is coming a day when every believer will stand before God to have his work judged. It will not determine whether or not you go to heaven. That is determined by your decision to be justified by the blood of Christ. But the judgment for your work will determine your reward.

God has an audit system. He will judge what you have built on the foundation of Jesus Christ. "Now if anyone builds on this foundation with gold, silver, precious stones, wood, hay, straw, each one's work will become clear; for the Day will declare it, because it will be revealed by fire; and the fire will test each one's work, of what sort it is" (1 Cor. 3:12–13).

When the fire burns up the wood, hay, and stubble, whatever remains will be rewarded. Some will be saved but have no reward for their works. It is important what you do in life to build the kingdom of God. Those who live quality lives in submission to the lordship of Christ will receive their reward. Compromise with the world will place your eternal reward in jeopardy.

Do you spend more time reading the Word of God or the TV guide? Are you fighting for your family or fighting with them? Do you sow generously in the kingdom or lay up treasure for yourself? To receive a white stone of *victory*, you have to live a life surrendered to doing the will of God.

Citizenship

The white stone had another significant meaning besides *justification* and *victory*. For foreigners who were not born in Pergamos, there was the possibility of achieving citizenship through their noble actions. If a person showed loyalty to the king, he could be given the most highly prized gift the city could bestow on a person: the white stone of citizenship.

With that coveted reward, a person was immediately adopted as a citizen with all the rights of those who were born in that city. As a believer in Jesus Christ, we have received the white stone of *citizenship* as our reward. Our names are written in the Book of Life, and we have all the privileges of a citizen of heaven.

FEAR FIGHTER

If you win the battle today, you will be promoted tomorrow.

Do you want to spend eternity with the Lord in heaven? Do you want to live forever in a place where the streets are paved with gold, mansions are the dwelling places of the redeemed, God is the light, and where love and peace rule? Can you imagine a place where there are no tears, no pain or sorrow or death (Rev. 21:4)? Are you making yourself eligible for such eternal rewards?

A WHITE STONE OR A WHITE THRONE?

Heaven is a real place. Hell is a real place. You have two options for living forever in your life after death. You have the option of receiving the *white stone* of reward in heaven when you overcome. And you have the option of receiving damnation before the *white throne* of judgment. What will your choice be—the white stone or the white throne?

The apostle John saw a great white throne that was the throne of God. And he saw all the dead standing before it. Then he saw books, including the Book of Life, opened before them. The dead were judged according to what they had done in life, which was written in the books. Anyone whose name was not recorded in the Book of Life was thrown into the lake of fire (Rev. 20:11–15).

You do not have to fear death or eternity when you have believed in Jesus to cleanse you of your sins. Your name is written in the Book of Life. You have only to live in anticipation of the day you will receive your reward. The apostle Paul said that to be absent from the body is to be present with the Lord (2 Cor. 5:8). When you die, you will live in eternal bliss in the very presence of God.

But Jesus Himself said to fear the one who had the power to cast you into hell. When you stand before the white throne judgment, you won't be able to plead your case. The guilty verdict is already in place if your name is not found in the Book of Life. That is based on your choice in life to reject Christ. Your eternal fate will be to be cast into the lake of fire with the devil and his angels.

You don't have to face that awful fate. I remember when I accepted Christ as my Savior. I walked into church knowing that I was a lost soul. I felt such guilt and condemnation when I heard the preached Word. Something inside of me said, "I can't take this anymore. I'm coming home to Jesus."

In that instant, Jesus came to me like the good Samaritan. He knelt over my wounded soul and poured in His healing oil. He picked me up and led me to safety and paid my debt. He took care of me until I was made whole. And He is still taking care of me. He said to the Father, "Just put everything that he needs on My account. I have paid the price for all his sin."

That is the good news of the gospel. Jesus has paid the penalty for your sin, your failure, your addiction. He wants you to call on His name so that He can heal your wounds and set you totally free. Jesus will justify you, make you victorious, and offer you citizenship in heaven as your eternal home. When you make Him Lord of your life, He releases you from all fear of eternity and replaces it with anticipation of your reward.

MAKING THE MOST OF THE "DASH"

Jesus affirmed the existence of heaven and hell in His teachings. And He showed us how to escape from eternal damnation by accepting His sacrifice for our sins. If you have done that, you will have no fear of eternity. When you have settled your eternal destiny, what matters most is what you do with the *dash*.

Carved into a tombstone, there is usually a name and then dates—a beginning date and an ending date. Between those dates there is a little dash. Have you ever thought about the significance of that little dash?

It is a fact that you have no control over that beginning date. You did not choose when to be born. And you do not control the ending date either. No one chooses when to die. But you do have control over the *dash* between those dates. The years between the beginning and ending dates—the dash—represent your life. You are living the dash. How are you doing with your dash?

FEAR FIGHTER

Choosing to become a *fear fighter* guarantees that you will be an overcomer in His kingdom.

The Word of God teaches you how to make your life on Earth most effective. After you accept Jesus as your Savior, God will reveal your personal destiny to you as you seek Him in prayer and in His Word. There is no greater joy, no greater liberty from the torment of fear, than when you learn to walk in the purpose of God for your life. That is when the *dash* becomes most effective and fulfilling. As a good steward of the gift of life God has given you, you will learn to build well on the foundation of Christ. And you will become eligible for the rewards of heaven He promises to those who overcome.

When your life is in the hands of Jesus Christ, death is not to be feared. He has the keys of death in His hands. For the fear fighter, death becomes simply a doorway to entering His presence, receiving your eternal reward, and living with Him forever and ever. You can overcome every fear that has tormented you when you surrender to His lordship.

If you want to experience glorious freedom from the fear of eternity, I encourage you to pray this prayer. As you do, you can expect to live a life totally free from fear:

> *Dear Lord Jesus, I accept forgiveness for my sins through the blood of Christ. And I give my life to You for Your*

purposes. I am determined to live as a fear fighter to establish the kingdom of God in my life, in my family, in the church, and in the world. Thank You for giving me the promise of my eternal reward and for delivering me from the fear of eternity. Through Your grace, I know that my name is written in the Book of Life and I will receive the white stone of the overcomer. Let me live in anticipation of my eternal home in heaven with You. Amen.

No Fear of Eternity

Let not your heart be troubled; you believe in God, believe also in Me. In My Father's house are many mansions...I go to prepare a place for you...I will come again and receive you to Myself.

—JOHN 14:1–3

Blessed be the God and Father of our Lord Jesus Christ, who according to His abundant mercy has begotten us again to a living hope through the resurrection of Jesus Christ from the dead.

—1 PETER 1:3

...that through death he might destroy him that had the power of death, that is, the devil; and deliver them who through fear of death were all their lifetime subject to bondage.

—HEBREWS 2: 14–15, KJV

We are confident, I say, and willing rather to be absent from the body, and to be present with the Lord.

—2 CORINTHIANS 5:8, KJV

I am He who lives, and was dead, and behold, I am alive forevermore. Amen. And I have the keys of Hades and of Death.

—REVELATION 1:18

My Personal Fear Fighters

_____

_____

_____

_____

_____

_____

_____

_____

_____

_____

_____

_____

_____

_____

_____

_____

_____

_____

My Fear Fighter Strategy

Now that you have finished reading this book, describe your action plan for fighting fear daily from this day forward.

_____

_____

_____

_____

_____

_____

_____

_____

_____

_____

_____

_____

_____

_____

NOTES

CHAPTER 1
FACING OFF WITH YOUR FEARS

1. Author unknown, "Risk," SermonIllustrations.com, http://www.sermonillustrations.com/a-z/r/risk.htm (accessed August 7, 2009).

CHAPTER 2
MUCH ADO ABOUT NOTHING

1. Harvey Mackay, "Worrying Makes You Cross the Bridge Before You Come to It," HarveyMackay.com, http://www.harvey mackay.com/columns/best/13.cfm (accessed August 10, 2009).

2. Melinda Beck, "When Fretting Is in Your DNA: Overcoming the Worry Gene," *Wall Street Journal*, January 15, 2008, http://online.wsj.com/public/article/SB120035992325490045-S7N NT9QSkUAcrtk71eF9iSTcapk_20090114.html?mod=rss_free (accessed August 10, 2009).

3. William Ralph Inge, "Famous Quotes and Authors," http://www.famousquotesandauthors.com/topics/worry_quotes.html (accessed August 10, 2009).

4. Deepak Chopra, "The Six Most Feared but Least Likely Causes of Death," SixWise.com, http://www.sixwise.com/newsletters/05/07/13/the_six_most_feared_but_least_likely_causes_of_death.htm (accessed May 13, 2009).

5. Norman J. Lund, "Why Study Shakespeare?," http://www.oxfordtutorials.com/why_study_shakespeare.htm (accessed August 10, 2009).

6. David M. Newman, *Sociology* (Thousand Oaks, CA: Pine Forge Press, 2008), 20.

7. Ibid.

8. Ibid.

9. The Quotations Page, "Dorothy Bernard Quotes," http://www.quotationspage.com/quote/29699.html (accessed August 10, 2009).

10. FutureHealth.org, "Courage Quotations," http://www.futurehealth.org/populum/pagesimple.php?f=Courage-Quotations-132 (accessed August 10, 2009).

CHAPTER 6
THE FEAR OF NOT HAVING ENOUGH

1. Amarnath Tewary, "India's Poor Urged to 'Eat Rats,'" BBCNews.com, http://news.bbc.co.uk/2/hi/south_asia/7557107.stm (accessed August 12, 2009).

CHAPTER 7
FIGHTING THE FEAR OF FAILURE

1. Child Development Institute, "Helping Your Child Deal With Fears and Phobias," http://www.childdevelopmentinfo.com/disorders/fears.htm (accessed August 13, 2009).

2. John Cook, Steve Deger, and Leslie Ann Gibson, *The Book of Positive Quotations*, (Minneapolis, MN: Fairview Press, 2007), 482.

3. BrainyQuote.com, "Thomas A. Edison Quotes," http://www.brainyquote.com/quotes/quotes/t/thomasaed132683.html (accessed August 13, 2009).

4. Jacques Pepin, "The Time 100: Ray Kroc," http://www.time.com/time/time100/builder/profile/kroc.html (accessed August 13, 2009).

5. Ron Kurtus, "Failures of Abraham Lincoln," School for Champions, http://www.school-for-champions.com/history/lincoln_failures.htm (accessed September 1, 2009).

6. "'Professor' Albert Einstein Unmasked At Last!" http://www.reformation.org/einstein-unmasked.html (accessed July 9, 2009).

7. "Sir Roger Bannister," Answers.com, http://www.answers.com/topic/roger-bannister (accessed July 9, 2009).

8. "Failure," Great-Quotes.com, http://www.great-quotes.com/cgi-bin/viewquotes.cgi?action=search&Category=Failure (accessed May 2, 2009).

9. "Biography of Nathaniel Hawthorne," GradeSaver.com, http://www.gradesaver.com/author/hawthorne (accessed July 9, 2009).

10. The butterfly effect is credited to Edward Lorenz and refers to scientific calculations that indicate the powerful effects of the minute change in airwaves produced by the flapping wings of a delicate butterfly. For more information see "Butterfly Effect," Answers.com, http://www.answers.com/topic/butterfly-effect-2 (accessed May 5, 2009).

11. Ibid.

12. Sir Winston Churchill, as cited in John Cook, Steve Deger, Leslie Ann Gibson, *The Book of Positive Quotations* (Minneapolis, MN: Fairview Press, 2007), 486.

13. "Lion," *Encarta Encyclopedia*, http://encarta.msn.com/encyclopedia_761566718/Lion.html (accessed May 7, 2009).

CHAPTER 8
OVERCOMING THE FEAR OF PEOPLE

1. Adapted from "Who's Your Daddy?" found on the Internet at http://www.mrwebauthor.com/mrmrswebauthor/forum/15.html (accessed July 17, 2009). Copyright © MrWebAuthor.com 2002-2006. Copyright © MrsWebAuthor.com 2005-2006. Copyright © LongLiveTechTV.com 2004-2006. All Rights Reserved. Wagoner, Oklahoma. U.S.A.

CHAPTER 9
NO FEAR OF ETERNITY

1. "Anxiety and Fear," Encyclopedia of Death and Dying, http://www.deathreference.com/A-Bi/Anxiety-and-Fear.html (accessed May 13, 2009).

2. Chopra, "The Six Most-Feared But Least Likely Causes of Death."

3. Sam Storms, "The Letter to the Church at Pergamum," Enjoying God Ministries, http://www.enjoyinggodministries .com/article/the-letter-to-the-church-at-pergamum-212-17/ (accessed July 29, 2009).